Leaving
My Amish World

Eirene Eicher

Dedication and Acknowledgements:

To my seven sons.

To my children and grandchildren whom I love more than life itself. Also to my parents and my brothers and sisters who remain very dear to my heart, who have helped shape the person I am today and who always will remain a part of my heart.

To the late Wm Gentry for his support and encouragement in the writing of this book up to the very last weeks of his life.

To my many supportive friends who have been my sounding board and have been there for me through every stage of the creation of this book and have offered encouragement, love and support. I love and appreciate each and every one of you very much. You all make life worth living.

Authors note:

Because of the nature of this story and everyone involved, names and places have been changed for the protection of everyone involved. My intent is not to hurt anyone but to bring awareness to someone who like me may be struggling or "stuck" in life and who could learn there is help available and find the courage to reach out or to prevent another young mother from all the pain that I've endured all these years.

Also please keep in mind all Amish communities have different customs and rules, and some in this book may not be what you are familiar with.

Other than the name changes and the place changes, this is my 100% true story.

***

All bible verses are from the King James Version Bible.

CONTENTS

CHAPTER 1 1

CHAPTER 2 7

CHAPTER 3 10

CHAPTER 4 16

CHAPTER 5 21

CHAPTER 6 26

CHAPTER 7 31

CHAPTER 8 37

CHAPTER 9 42

CHAPTER 10 46

CHAPTER 11 52

CHAPTER 12 57

CHAPTER 13 61

CHAPTER 14 65

CHAPTER 15 69

CHAPTER 16 74

CHAPTER 17 79

CHAPTER 18 83

ABOUT THE AUTHOR 89

Chapter 1

Leaving my Amish world was excruciatingly painful, to put it mildly. It was the toughest decision I would ever make.

I love my Amish family. They are my world. The only one I've ever known. My heritage! How could I ever make such a harsh, drastic decision?

On my own it would've been impossible. I couldn't bear the thought of hurting my parents. It would be very hard on them to find out that I was no longer following in the traditions they had taught me. It was very hard on not only them but on me, my husband, and children as well. And for that I am very sorry.

On my own, I never would have chosen to leave. I never ever meant to hurt them or any of my beloved siblings whom I love very deeply. Some of the dearest people in the world to me are my siblings, and it tears my heart out not to share my world with them: My joys and sorrows, the birth of my babies, the triumphs and struggles. The victories of my children.

Will they ever know my boys? I surely hope so. I did not leave the Amish faith for any other reason than God leading me in the direction He wanted me to go.

He has an individual walk for each person. I left all that I ever knew to follow Him. He may not require this path for everyone but it was the path He chose for me. He tells me in His Word that if I'm not willing to forsake all to follow Him, then I am not worthy of Him.

As a young girl growing up, I loved to read books. We didn't have the screens, the tech toys that children have today, but we had books and I read many of them. They took me to another world.

I would read for hours on end, sometimes long into the night I would read by my oil lamp, long after everyone else was asleep. I would read many different genres of books. One in particular that was gripping and life-changing was reading about the Anabaptists where my forefathers originated from back in the 1600's.

I read how they would have to hide their Bibles and go underground to have their church services, and if they were found out it meant certain death, but that did not stop them. Many did get caught and went willingly to be burned at the stake. They would sing unto their death. They loved the Lord with a fierce undying love.

I wanted that kind of faith and I began to wonder where it had gotten lost. I didn't see it in the churches today but I wanted it.

All Amish communities are different, and many do teach that God is loving and you can have a close personal relationship with him, but my community did not teach that. They taught that God was strict and critical, and that we had to follow our long list of man-made rules in order to get into heaven.

Little did I know that all I had to do was believe in and love the Lord in order to get into heaven. I was taught good works would get me into heaven. I was taught I had to be "good enough."

I wanted more than a form of godliness. I wanted to serve a living God. I wanted much more than to follow rules set in the church letter.

I will take a minute to explain that there are many different sects of Amish. Each sect has their own set of rules, better known as the church letter. No two sects are exactly alike. For example, some may allow buttons on their clothes while others considered them to be too prideful. Some may allow indoor plumbing, bicycles, motors, or generators while others consider that to be worldly. If we wanted some of the more modern conveniences, we had to move into a church district where it was allowed.

Where I come from, I was taught that if I followed the church letter and lived a good life, I had hope to make it to heaven. My perception of God was that he was way out there somewhere far away. I believed he was in heaven looking down to see what I did wrong and writing it in his big black book. I did not know him on a personal level, but I wanted to.

However, I enjoyed growing up in the Amish community. I have two older brothers who are thirteen months older than me. I loved following them around all over the place down the cow path to bring the cows in for milking, to cleaning out the pig pens (a stinky job), and up to the hayloft to throw down the hay bales, which usually ended with us swinging from one loft to the other hanging onto the long thick ropes.

I did all this wearing my little Amish dress since girls were not allowed to wear pants, but it was still so much fun. The twins are 13 months older than me, so they got to go to school while I stayed behind. I remember those days vividly. After they got on the bus, my sisters and I had to do the dishes. At that time, I was not fond of the task. There were days when we lolly-gagged, doing dishes all day long. We would still be doing dishes when the boys got off the bus in the afternoon.

I remember washing the dishes as my sister dried them and I would tease her mercilessly. I knew just what to say to push her buttons and she would chase me around all over the house and out the door, calling out to mom, who was busy at the sewing machine or whatever other countless things a busy mother had to do.

I laughed while she cried. I am sure I owe her a huge apology. She knew I loved her, and for the most part, we got along great. As we got older, we became best friends.

My sisters and I loved each other, and often times we would play house out in the hayloft. We would use the hay bales to create partitions and make them into 'rooms'. And one of us would be dad and another the mom, and of course the rest were the kids.

We always had an abundance of cats and kittens on the farm, and we would dress the little kitties in doll clothes and pretend they were our babies. It was hard trying to get them to sit still while having our pretend church service.

We got along well and these times were fun and enjoyable. I absolutely adored my older brothers and they didn't seem to mind me trailing along behind them. Sometimes they would ask me to choose which one of the two I liked the best. Of course, I couldn't choose one over the other. I dearly loved them both. And absolutely loved all the fun times we had together.

I also shared their love of all our animals, especially the horses. I was the oldest girl which meant I would shoulder a lot of the workload in the house, helping my mom. It seemed there was always a lot of work with our fast-growing family.

Every other year there was another baby and as I got older, my mom would deliver the babies at home and I got to clean them up and dress them in the new baby gowns. My mom used to say, "I wish I had two Eirenes," which made me feel very much needed.

Growing up in a big family didn't give me much free time, but I enjoyed every free minute I did get. I'd go for a walk, ride horses, or read my books. I passionately loved doing all of those activities. Sometimes my brothers and I would walk over to the neighbors and watched as they milked the cows and did their chores. It was enjoyable to watch as they poured bucket after bucket of the rich milk into the strainers which they set up over five-gallon galvanized cans. They'd set the cans into cement tanks with cold water to keep them the right temperature until the milkman would come pick them up. Even the cleanup was fun to watch.

As we got older and my sisters were old enough to share the workload, we also learned quickly the art of cooking. Lots and lots of cooking. This is an art that doesn't come easy for a lot of young girls today and one that I just took for granted, but in our Amish culture it was not option.

That's just what girls did in my community. We learned to cook and run a household. I just thought all girls know how to cook. So we girls worked alongside our mom who was always known for her "good cooking."

Today I greatly appreciate all that my mother taught me. I soon learned how to whip up a big meal in minutes and still do to this day. Our scrumptious mashed potatoes and gravy, buttered homemade noodles, home-grown sweet corn or green beans fresh from the garden, delicious chicken fried to perfection, sirloin beef tip roast with gravy or pork chops browned and baked with mushrooms.

The more complicated dishes such as casseroles we learned to make from scratch, not using recipes, which can seem like either a blessing or a curse. They can be a blessing because we memorize the recipes in our mind, or they can be a curse since we don't have exact measurements on recipe cards which makes it difficult to pass on to others.

My dad enjoyed listening to us girls sing, yodel, and play the harmonica. When family friends would come over, he would ask us to do it for them too. There were times when we weren't willing to sing, so he would promise us gifts for doing it, and sure enough he'd come home from work the next day with nice little gifts for us.

Chapter 2

One thing we learned as Amish kids growing up is the value of good, strong work ethic. We worked hard and learned to enjoy it too. There was never a shortage of things to do. If we weren't cooking, baking, canning, sewing, or ironing, then we were tending a garden, mowing the lawn, or painting buggies and fences.

We not only worked hard, but played hard too. The day came when I was old enough to start school. We as Amish do not have kindergarten; we start our school years in first grade.

I soon learned that I loved school. I had a hunger for knowledge, for learning new things, reading, writing, and spelling. What I liked more than anything was recess time where we would go outside and play games like Round Town (a form of softball), Kick the Can, and Peek Around the Corner. On rainy days we'd play in the basement.

One game we played down there was called Keep Away. It consisted of two teams and one football, and I remember very well one day while playing this game that I got hit in the stomach with the ball and passed out. It knocked the air out of me. Needless to say, I was done for the day but I didn't have the luxury of going to the nurse's office because we didn't have one. And there were no phones, so we couldn't call mom to come pick me up. Even if we could have it would've taken most of the day for her to catch the horse, hitch it up, and drive to the school.

And so I toughed it out until the end of the day. Most of the time a driver with a big van would pick up all the Amish kids and take them to their schools.

Even though there were a lot of Amish kids that got on the bus and went to a public school, we never did. We always went to the private Amish Parochial Schools which in the earlier years were taught by an English (non-Amish) person who was certified to teach school. But in my later years, our teachers were all Amish teachers.

Our schools consisted of a one-room schoolhouse with eight grades all in one room. There were approximately twenty to twenty-six students per school room. There is usually one school per church district. And so whenever we wanted to change churches, we actually had to move to the district that church was in, which meant changing schools. As a child I had to do this three times.

The last school I attended was taught by several different teachers throughout my years there. At times we had two teachers at the same time, one for the younger students and another for the older grades. Finally, in my last couple years, my teacher was my uncle who was also the bishop of the church I attended.

I soon learned that I was at the top of the class along with my first cousin Noah. We always had our studies done before everyone else. He would do a lot of drawing in his free time while I read my beloved books. At one of our parent teacher meetings I overheard the teacher talking to my mom about me as her student and suggested that I could skip a grade if I wanted to.

I knew I didn't want to skip a grade. I wanted to experience each grade I possibly could since we were only allowed an eighth grade education. I loved school and wanted to learn all that I possibly could. There were many times when we as students who were all caught up with our studies were asked to help the teachers teach or even help a student who was struggling to catch up. I had the experience of being a substitute teacher even while I was attending school. I especially enjoyed helping my friends who struggled or had learning disabilities. It was fulfilling to see the light bulb come on as they learned new things and improved their grades.

Summertime was equally as fun, especially the times when my dad would take the whole family to fun places. He seemed to love life and every summer he would take us to the lakes or somewhere fun. I remember times when he would be doing some construction work for a farmer who owned a big stock truck with an open back end. It could hold as many as thirty people. We along with several of Dad's workers and their families would pile into the back of the truck and go off to the lakes. We'd go swimming, riding speed boats, and having picnics. Dad knew how to make life fun. We all enjoyed these fun outings.

It was always a pleasure to go to work with Dad. Many, many times he needed all the help he could get when he was doing work for chicken farmers. They needed as many hands as they could find to help carry the chickens and load them into crates on big semi-trucks.

We always knew that we would get to eat in a real sit-down restaurant where we could order whatever food we wanted after helping him. This usually included one of my favorites which was French fries. This was always the highlight of the day and made work seem like fun.

My dad did a lot of construction and remodeling work as well as build new pole barns, and so at a young age he would take some of us kids along with him to work. It wasn't long until my brothers and I would ask to help run the screw guns as he hung the sheets of metal for siding. We learned many things like this at a very young age.

Chapter 3

By the time I was a teenager we had grown into a large family which shifted responsibilities and us older kids. We started to have jobs of our own. I remember the first babysitting job I had at the age of 14, which required me to stay a week at a time. This was new to me. I had never been away from home for more than a night or two at a time, and so a whole week was almost unbearable.

I remember crying myself to sleep at night in bed and counted the days when I could go home again. In the daytime it was easier because I kept busy and also had television to watch, something new for me since we didn't have electricity or any modern conveniences. I would soon find myself getting hooked on soap operas. I still remember some of them like The Guiding Light or Days of Our Lives. It didn't take long for me to get all wrapped up in TV drama.

Both my parents came from large families and I adored my aunts. It was always a treat for me to spend time with aunt Barbara, my mom's sister. She and her husband always made me feel welcome and wanted. They had tried to have children but it just wasn't happening, so I was extra close to aunt Barbara.

She was always happy, always smiling or laughing. It was such a fun time at their house where we would get into their swimming pool after a hot day in the field. I'll never forget the blistering sunburn on my back on one of those occasions when I stayed in the pool too long. That was very painful. It hurt so bad I could hardly sleep at night.

Aunt Barbara adored her husband. She worked in the barn and fields alongside him. They had a big barn full of farm animals, horses, sheep, cows, pigs and chickens. She would always allow me to gather the eggs from the hen house. I can still hear the squawking of the chickens as we shooed them out of their nests to gather their eggs. They didn't seem to appreciate us taking their eggs from them and then there was always a rowdy rooster or two in the bunch. They sometimes made me nervous as they would fight each other and chase us out of the chicken coop.

One advantage to spending time at my aunt's house was that I had their undivided one-on-one attention, since they didn't have children of their own, something I wasn't used to. I loved it very much when they would take an interest in me and my life, and not only talk to me, but listen to what I had to say. It made me feel loved and heard and cared for.

I often wondered what it would have been like to be an only child, and staying with my aunt and uncle kind of gave me an idea. I concluded it has its advantages and disadvantages. I was always very happy to go back home to my siblings where there was never a dull moment.

At the age of sixteen is when we as young Amish people start our "rumspringa" or going out with the crowd days. I eagerly anticipated joining my older brothers who had been going for a year already and seemed to be having so much fun. I always enjoyed listening to them as they discussed the events that happened, like who took beautiful Sarah home for a date, or how Sam who wanted Sarah but she turned him down for the tall, handsome Jake. And about all the fun times. They would talk about Johnny's fast horse or David's shiny new buggy with the hidden speakers under the seat, which was totally forbidden. David liked to live life on the wild side.

Having any musical instruments was against the rules of the church except for the harmonica. Lots of our young people are quite accomplished harmonica players, some extremely talented. This was one of the joys of a Sunday night crowd, listening to the harmonica players along with the singing and yodeling. There was nothing more fun on a summer night, especially when the party was taking place out in a barn where the floor had been cleared for dancing or the "Huddleshtrow," as it was called in our language. We would partner up and dance long into the night.

Many times, I'd wake up on a Monday morning with sore, aching arms but I didn't mind. The fun we had was totally worth any pain I endured.

I enjoyed sharing with my younger sisters the events of the crowds. They were not yet old enough to go to the crowds. So when Monday morning came, I would relate stories to them as we did our chores or laundry or whatever task we were assigned. They listened with anticipation as I told them about being asked out by whomever it was the night before or as I talked about the fun we had playing "Huddleshtrow." They could hardly wait until they could join me in the fun.

In our Amish culture, the young people were expected to start following church at the age of sixteen in order to become members. If for some reason they decided they weren't ready at that age, they were considered rebellious.

An Amish young couple could not get married until they were members. That is also when the guys were required to start growing their beards. In many Amish communities only married men have beards, but not where I'm from.

For the most part, the majority of the young folks would comply with the church rules without rebelling or questioning the reasons why. We had always been discouraged to ask too many questions about our faith.

We were always told, "That's just the way we've been taught," or "Who are we to question what our forefathers taught us?" And so I was content to follow the traditions of our forefathers.

Growing up with in a big family of fourteen kids was interesting and fun. There were many unforgettable moments. One Friday night in particular was an unforgettable experience. It was when a new law passed for slow-moving vehicles to display a red triangle emblem on the back of the buggy for reflection. After we had enjoyed our evening in town, we were on our way home when a police officer pulled us over for not having the required emblem.

When the officer confronted my dad, his reply was, "I thought that was just for slow-moving vehicles!"

"Yes, you're right," replied the officer.

Dad replied, "Well, this isn't a slow-moving vehicle. My horse can run at 30 mph. I will prove it. You can clock me."

And he did prove it! My dad had the horse running as fast as it could go with the officer driving behind us. Finally the officer pulled up alongside the buggy and called out to my dad and said, "She was up there, she was flying!"

It seemed my dad could talk his way out of almost anything. The farm life was the best. I never got tired of the smell of fresh-cut hay in the fields or the glory of early-morning sunrise, the warmth of it as I did my early morning chores before going inside to cook breakfast for everyone. Life was so simple. So uncomplicated.

We didn't have television, radio, or even electricity. I think that's one of the things I miss the most. The simple, uncomplicated life in the country where we found joy in the simple things. It didn't take a lot of money since we grew our own vegetables in the garden and butchered our own meats. I remember many times helping my mom pluck the feathers from the chickens for company coming to dinner.

Our family always pitched in and worked together at our annual hog butchering day. We'd all get together very early on a cold winter day with family and neighbors. The guys would build a hot fire under the cast-iron kettles to scald the hogs. We womenfolk would work hard to prepare a huge delicious meal for the hungry crew. There were always hot, delicious and scrumptious foods including home-made pies, cakes, doughnuts, rolls, and warm bread with melted butter. Yum!

Butchering was an all-day affair. Long, tiring hours of cutting up the meat, making sausage, stuffing it into casings. We always looked forward to the cracklings or pork rinds as we call them today and also the popcorn that was popped in the kettle after all the meat was done up. No one left hungry. Tired maybe, but not hungry. Butchering day was long and exhausting, but the benefits of having smoked ham, sausage, and canned meats readily available all year long was worth all the hard work.

Another memory I have as a kid is going to grandma and grandpa's farm to spend the day. I loved following my grandpa out to the barn where my uncles milked the cows. It was fun to watch as they squirted milk into the cat's mouths, poking fun at each other. Sometimes they sang and yodeled as they milked the cows or did their chores. I still remember grandpa sitting there, puffing on his tobacco pipe. I loved the smell of it and the laid-back atmosphere. I don't ever remember him being in a hurry about anything.

He loved working with wood and making things like little wagons and wooden toys. He along with my uncles would also make the wooden caskets when someone passed away in the Amish community. These were just simple wooden caskets with a very distinctive, unforgettable smell of pine wood coated with polyurethane varnish. I'll always cherish the memories of fun times at grandpa and grandma's house.

The food was always scrumptious. My grandma cooked everything in aluminum and cast-iron pots and pans. She served food on mismatched dinnerware and chipped saucers. They lived very frugally. I remember my mom telling us that she never knew what hamburger was. She was seventeen when she tasted her first hamburger. But my relatives were rich in other areas of life. Like when we would have a big family get-together and my uncles would sing and yodel. They were very talented and it was a real treat to sit and listen to them harmonize. They always sang acapella and never played instruments. It was so beautiful. I will cherish those memories forever.

Chapter 4

In our culture, the kids work and help earn a living for the family. We were required to give our paychecks to our parents until we reached the accountability age of twenty-one or until we would get married, whichever came first. We never knew anything different, and so when I turned sixteen, my parents got me a job working in the kitchen at the local bar in town. Even though I enjoyed cooking, I did not like this job. I vowed I'd never ask a child of my own to work at a bar.

My parents knew the owners and they needed good kitchen help. I felt like I was cooking food for a bunch of dirty old men. Whenever I would take the freshly washed shot glasses back to the bar, there were always guys sitting there drinking and wanting to flirt with the little Amish girl. I remember feeling 'dirty' as their eyes feasted on me. Tommy the bar owner would always give me a handful of quarters and ask me to go play the jukebox because I knew all the good songs to play. Thankfully this job didn't last very long. It was in this same timeframe that I began rumspringa.

I have seen so much drunkenness. Alcoholism runs rampant in our community. Not only in my immediate family but in my extended family, my uncles, and in my community in general. This is another way that my community was different than many Amish communities, because most Amish communities forbid alcohol.

This was the way I was raised. In literally everything we did alcohol was involved. In family gatherings, in afternoon cookouts, during a Sunday church service in the basement, at neighborhood cattle or hog butchering events. Any time there was a function there was a reason to drink.

Though it was a taboo subject, and there are many Amish communities where sex before marriage is strictly forbidden, but it was not forbidden where I came from.

At the end of the evening, often the guys would ask a girl for a date which consisted of him taking her home in the horse and buggy and would end with him taking her up to her room. No one ever talked to me about abstinence or even gave me the "birds and the bees" talk. The subject of sex was something "dirty" that we were not allowed to discuss.

No wonder there were so many "shotgun" weddings, a term used when a girl became pregnant and was forced to marry the guy who impregnated her regardless of whether or not they were in love. If he got her pregnant, he was obligated to marry her. These were some of the things I never understood, even to this day.

My rumspringa days were very short lived. Less than a year after joining the "crowd," I became pregnant by the guy I dated, Mark, so I had to marry him. We figured it was the right thing to do. My parents were not happy about it but did not object. So at the tender young age of seventeen I was a pregnant, married woman. There are not a lot of happy memories of my wedding day. Right before the ceremony, Mark whispered in my ear, "You can still back out."

I was very tempted to do so. But where would I go? What would I do? A pregnant unmarried Amish girl was a disgrace. How would I make it in life with no education and no husband? The fear of the unknown was greater than my not wanting to get married. We continued on with the wedding proceedings.

The Amish wedding ceremony was very similar to a traditional Amish church service except that we along with our witnesses sat in front of the preachers who would conduct the ceremony. It was a cool spring day and I was nervous as we sat in silence listening to the hymnals being sung. Then the opening preacher began to deliver his sermon, admonishing us to stay true to the church and to each other. Everything felt so surreal as I listened to the traditional words being spoken. I felt invisible but I was obedient. I was going through the motions, doing what was expected of me. Never considering my own thoughts, emotions or opinions.

I always felt like I had no choice in anything that I did. After exchanging our vows it was time to go back home to my parents' house where the wedding supper was being held. I was overwhelmed by all the people that came to the wedding. There were at least five hundred guests. My parents spared no expense for the wedding. I was the first of my family to be married and they did it right. There was so much food and alcohol. We did what most of the young couples do and that is provide food and drink. In fact, Mark was drunk on our wedding night. It was disheartening from day one.

I remember drinking beer from the time I was sixteen years old. I went from being told what to do and living in obedience to my parents to living in obedience and submission to my husband. I never knew who I really was, but thankfully I enjoyed being a stay-at-home mom. That is still what I would've chosen had I been given a choice—it was what I absolutely loved to do. I was excited about having a baby of my own. I vowed I would love and protect the precious little human being created inside of me.

I was hoping he would be a boy. I liked the idea of the oldest child being a boy. He was all mine and I couldn't wait to hold him. Mark and I were both young when we got married. He was twenty and I was seventeen. We had very little to set up a household since we had to give our paychecks to our parents. There wasn't any reserve money. No savings accounts or anything like that. I gave my parents my paycheck until about a week or so before the wedding. It was required until we are twenty-one years old or when we get married, whichever comes first. My husband used to jokingly say that was the reason he got married just to keep his own paycheck.

I remember our first trip to the grocery store. I needed so much but was afraid to ask my husband how much money I was allowed to spend for groceries. It was at the old IGA in Indiana.

I got the bare necessities on that first trip. I knew I could count on my mom to help me with whatever I didn't buy since we lived in the little adjoining summer house at my parents' home. That was one of the requirements. In order for them to give permission and sign papers to allow me to get married, I had to promise to live in the summer house because my mom needed my help with the rest of her children. So we did.

Our marriage was rocky right from the start. My life seemed to spiral out of control into a chaotic environment. I loved my husband when he was sober, but when he was drunk, he turned into something else. I hadn't signed up for that. I had always imagined my own home to be a safe place where my husband and I would raise our children in love and unity. I would never have chosen to raise my children in such an unstable home, but what did I know? I was merely a child myself.

I was only a woman. In my community, I was expected to keep quiet and be submissive and obedient. Like my uncle once told me, "As long as he puts the bread and butter on the table, you need to keep your mouth shut." Cruel words, but I did.

I worked very hard, not only to keep our humble abode neat, but cooking for my husband while also helping my mom raise my siblings, working in the garden, and sewing everything that goes along with housekeeping for my mom as well as my own work, all while being pregnant and having morning sickness from the pregnancy.

Really? This was the life of newly-weds? Where was the love, joy, wedded bliss or even a honeymoon? I went from being a hardworking submissive daughter to a hardworking submissive housewife. I did not have the luxury or the experience of being a carefree teenager.

I was always just a "mommy". I never got to live life for me or make my own decisions. I was always told what to do, how to think, what clothes I could or could not wear. No one ever asked me what I wanted to do or what my feelings, thoughts, or opinions were about anything. I worked very hard to please everyone in my world, everyone except myself. The days and weeks and months passed. My due date was fast approaching.

One day at my regular scheduled appointments the doctor told me I had the option of my labor being induced, since he would be on vacation the following week, and I had already begun to dilate. I was ready and agreed to do it.

Before I went to the hospital, I tried to reach my husband and ask him to meet me there. He was working on a construction crew and I could not reach him. So off to the hospital I went to have my first baby alone.

As they prepared me for labor, I was both excited and scared, wishing my husband was there. Meanwhile on the job, my husband started to feel like something was wrong at home. Call it a premonition, intuition, or sympathy pains.

Whatever it's called was strong enough to make him go home where he found the baby bed all prepared with my note for him to come to the hospital. He rushed to be by my side but didn't end up coming into the labor room. He just couldn't stand it, so he stayed outside until little Sebastian made his appearance into this world.

Chapter 5

I was ecstatic to have my first baby boy. He was so beautiful. He had lots of black hair. My world was complete. My husband and I were both excited to have our little Sebastian join us and looked forward to taking him home. We were so proud of our beautiful baby boy. We were so protective of him and wouldn't allow too many people come in to our home to hold him.

We soon learned he had his days and nights mixed up. He would sleep all day long and was awake during the night. Every two hours he'd want to eat. Needless to say, I was a very tired, sleep deprived, young seventeen-year-old-mother. And life was getting very hectic with each passing day.

I found great joy in taking care of my little boy. He was so perfect. Lots of dark hair, brown eyes and rosy cheeks. He had such a sweet disposition and I thoroughly enjoyed taking care of him. He made me a mother and I found motherhood to be fulfilling and enjoyable.

My days were very full and consisted of changing diapers and feeding him. Doing laundry and dishes became a never-ending job. Not only was I busy with my little household, but also still helping my mom which was a job in itself. There was never a shortage of things that had to be done. Monday morning—washday—was a big job. We hand carried every drop of water into the house which we had to heat on our kerosene stove. We then poured it into our hand-operated washing machine and then hand wrung it into another tub to rinse and one last time before hanging it out on clothesline. This was a two-day job, especially in the winter when the clothes would freeze. It was so much easier to pack the piles of laundry into baskets and tubs and hire a driver to take us to the laundromat. At least that would allow us to finish the laundry in one day.

There were also the days when we needed to do the ironing, sewing, baking, cooking, and cleaning. There was never an end to household chores, but doing it with family made it so much easier and much more fun as well.

I loved the camaraderie I had with my sisters. We enjoyed working together and to just be in each other's company. I never thought that would ever come to an end.

We did everything together: working, playing, singing, or just visiting. We were very close-knit and had strong family bonds which at the time I thought were unbreakable.

Having grown up in the Amish culture taught me strong family values. I loved my family, and the thought of ever leaving the security of my Amish world never crossed my mind.

I was quite content going to church once every other week. It was tradition. We were taught that by our forefathers and we were not to question their teachings. And so I didn't. I was content to do as I was told.

Many, many times I would wonder what meaning my life had on this earth. I would ask myself, was this really all God put me on this earth for? Just to have babies? Just to be a wife? To follow the church letter? What was the meaning of all this? Where was the passion for the things of God like I had read about in the *Book of Martyrs*?

These were questions I just could not find answers to. When I'd read my German Bible looking for answers, things just didn't make sense because I could not understand the dialect it was written in. We were not to read the English Bible because in their words, and I quote, "The English Bible is too misleading and makes salvation sound just way too easy."

We were taught that the way to go to heaven was do as our forefathers taught us: Follow the church letter, be good people.

Do as the church taught us. Stay within the parameters and hope we would be good enough to go to heaven. I had very little assurance that I could ever be good enough, but boy, I tried!

As weeks turned into months and months into years, life became increasingly difficult as we continued to live a very dysfunctional life which at the time I believed to be 'normal'. But there were just so many nagging questions about who I was and who was I really supposed to be. What was the purpose for living? Had God really just put me here to cook, clean, do dishes, and be pregnant, as most of us Amish women were led to believe? Some even call themselves baby machines.

Mark went to work for my dad and we started planning a home of our own somewhere other than my parents' summer house which only had only two rooms—two small rooms at that. We definitely needed a real home to raise our family in. So we decided to buy a plot of land from Mark's parents and build a basement house.

It was exciting to make plans for our very first home. We took out a mortgage and built a small basement house with no indoor plumbing or electricity. We also had a barn built, and by this time I was pregnant with our second child.

Living next door to my mother-in-law was trouble from the very beginning. The alcoholism continued to get worse, therefore the emotional and verbal abuse turned physical, and of course the in-laws were on Mark's side and not mine.

I felt so alone, like a whole army was against me, and I had a child to protect and another on the way.

Feeling alone and stuck was an understatement.

As the drinking got worse, the physical fights escalated. And so my relationship with my husband and his family deteriorated.

But I had nowhere to go. We as Amish did not believe in divorce, and even if we did, I had no education, no transportation, no phone, nothing.

I was so stuck.

Life continued on and being a mother to little Sebastian who was the highlight of my life. His happy, outgoing personality was my sunshine. The innocence of my little boy and the love I felt for him made life worth living. He in his young baby years did not understand the pain and turmoil in this life. Not yet anyway. In our culture we were taught that using birth control was a sin and so I quickly became pregnant again for baby number two by this time I was eighteen years old.

It was winter time with snow and cold, so it became more difficult for me to lug in the wood and coal to feed the fire in our little stove. Since we lived in a basement house, it didn't take a lot to heat it up quickly. Only the front of our home was exposed to the cold, the rest of the 3 sides were built into the hill. We were very well protected from the heat of the summer as well as the snow and cold of the brutal winter of 1978, but it was also a detriment.

The snow was coming down hard and fast as we went to bed that cold January evening, but we had no idea that it would completely bury our basement home. The next morning when we got up, we discovered that we were snowed in and could not get out our front door. The snow had piled up at least ten feet deep.

We didn't know what to do. What if we had an emergency? We had no phone, no communication with the outside world. After breakfast was over, daylight came, and Mark decided to climb out the back-bedroom window which was barely big enough for a grown up to squeeze through.

He went to our good English neighbors who helped him find someone with a snowmobile to rescue us and take us to my in-laws' house one at a time. It was hard for this pregnant mama to squeeze myself through the little basement window, but not impossible. I knew I had to get myself out of there one way or another. This was an unforgettable experience. One I hoped would never happen again.

Mark, his dad, and several other guys found someone with a backhoe-like machine to create an opening to our front door. It felt like we were inside a tunnel as we walked between the 10-foot tall walls of snow to get inside the house. We found this was a big drawback to living in a basement house.

Chapter 6

It was May of '78 when baby number two was born. He was a beautiful healthy baby with lots of black hair and beautiful dark eyes. Now I had two sons who depended on me for everything and I totally loved being their mother. They brought happy times and sunshine into my life.

Along with that came more responsibility as well. I felt grateful for them in my life and thankful for the opportunity to raise them, even though I had very little to offer them materially speaking. But I was very rich in love.

Mothering my children was one thing I knew how to do, and I did it well. I lived one day at a time. It was all I could do. Thinking too far into the future was just too overwhelming. Although there were some fun, pleasant days, there was always that looming black cloud overhead.

I never knew when another drunken outburst of anger was going to happen. It was like walking on eggshells, never knowing what would set it off.

I always believed Mark when he said it was my fault he drank. It seemed like everything that went wrong was always my fault or at least someone other than his own. I never saw him take responsibility for his own actions. He always played the blame game. And my young naïve self-accepted the blame.

How I wished things were different. Why? Why? Why?

Mark seemed to enjoy working and he worked very hard. There was hardly ever a day of work that he missed for any reason. That is one of the things I admire about our Amish community. They taught us great work ethic and also to love doing it. Laziness was not in our vocabulary. We worked hard and we loved it.

No one could ever accuse Mark of being lazy. He would get up early and go off to work, leaving me to my world of being mom to my boys, which was most enjoyable to me. When I was alone in my world, I could be myself, which was a relief—however short lived it might be.

It wasn't until later on in life that I learned this was forbidden in other sects of Amish. I had always thought it was the norm.

At this point in our marriage, his drunken episodes happened mostly on weekends or whenever we would get together with family and friends. Drinking seemed to be the entertainment of choice for the guys in our sect of the Amish community. This was typical of the sect that I grew up in.

These were dreaded times for me as myself and the boys would be dropped off at one house and the menfolk would go off somewhere to drink. We moms were left to deal with all the kids who would play until dark, then they were hungry and tired, wanting to go home to bed, and I had no way to get them home by myself.

Myself along with the other moms were at the mercy of the guys and their drinking. Hour after hour would drag by with no sign of them. We didn't have phones so we couldn't call them, so we had no choice but to wait and wait and wait. I was so stuck.

Feelings of hopelessness engulfed me as I lived day-to-day life. It seemed I was not in control of anything at all. I didn't even feel like a wife. I was married and had children, but there was no companionship, no looking forward to sharing life, love, or emotional and spiritual connection with my husband. Isn't that what a marriage was supposed to be? I simply lived life as I was told and went through the emotions of everyday living:

Keeping the house clean and tidy, raising my boys, cooking, laundry, gardening, canning.

The list of chores was literally endless. Besides all that, I had to carry in every drop of water that I needed to do all of these chores as well as bath water. This was very hard and a lot of work, but it was the only way I knew. What was the meaning to all this unsettling chaotic life? How I longed for my simpler, less complicated life at home with my parents and siblings.

Eventually we decided to sell our basement house and we bought a house about a mile or so from my parents. Now I could walk to parents' house with my 2 babies and enjoy time with mom and my sisters. I absolutely loved the days we got to visit and do things together.

It didn't matter if we were making home-made noodles or canning a big batch of fresh vegetable soup, or just hanging out. It was a safe place for me. I felt loved and protected by my family. I still miss those days.

Mark seemed to like our new home. It was a farm home. A great place to raise our sons. A big house and also a little summer house. A summer house is a little house next to the home where all the cooking and canning is done in the summertime to keep the heat out of the main home.

Since we do not have air conditioning to cool our homes, a summer house is usually just outside the front door. We also had a big barn in a nice yard, so much bigger than our little basement home. A nice place for a little Amish family. We enjoyed having company and serving lots of home-cooked meals.

Cooking seemed to be one of my talents, and I dearly loved it. Serving seemed to be my lot in life. I served my family as a child, changing diapers for my siblings at the tender age of seven years old. And by the time I was twelve, I was doing everything a grown woman would do as far as running a household. I was babysitting, cooking, baking, cleaning, sewing, painting walls. There wasn't much I couldn't do.

And now as a married woman, I found myself serving my husband and children. In my mind that was my purpose in life. Isn't that what us Amish women were supposed to do? Serve our families?

My siblings also were getting married one by one. My older twin brothers dated sisters and soon they got married and started having children too. It was interesting to watch as the family dynamics changed and grew. As they had children, I now became an aunt and my little boys became cousins.

My boys grew close to their cousins since they got to spend so much time together at our weekly visits as my sisters and I continued to go home to my mom's to spend the day. They loved going out to the farm where they could run and play to their hearts' content. It made me happy to see them happy. How I wondered what life had in store for them.

Day by day as life went on, I would often wonder what the meaning of life was. So many times I would ask that million-dollar question: What is the meaning of life? Why am I here? Did our great big God really put me here just to live a mundane life? Every day the same thing over and over? To cook breakfast, do dishes, make the beds, sweep the floors, plan the next meal, and tend to the needs of everyone?

Is God really just way up there somewhere with his big black book, keeping track of all my sins, mistakes and transgressions? Or does he have a bigger plan for me? Is there a specific purpose for my life on earth? Is life meant to be such a painful struggle? Or is this just way it is supposed to be for insignificant little women like me?

Maybe this was all that I deserved. How I longed for a deeper relationship, a spiritual connection with God as well as my husband. There just had to be more to life than this.

My mind would often go back to the stories I read as a young girl about the Anabaptist people that had such a passion for Christ. The love, peace and joy they felt. God's glory would literally shine on their faces as they were being led to their death. They would even sing praises to God while being burnt at the stake. They had so much love for a savior they had never seen. This was beyond my comprehension. But I longed for that kind of living hope and peace. In all the years of my Amish life I could not find it.

Chapter 7

There were many nice times as I raised my boys. I poured my heart into them. They were my life, they were my whole world. Every waking moment revolved around them. I wanted so much more for them than I ever had in life.

I wanted a proper education for them which I never had. I wanted them to grow up into happy, healthy young men, making healthy choices, living happy, healthy lives. Being free to be all they could be.

Was there such a thing as that? I believed somewhere, somehow there was. If only their dad was more interested in them and their future! He could have been such a role model. Every son needs a loving father who is proud of his boys and leads by example. That's pretty hard to do for a dad who is drunk every weekend.

Winter, spring, summer, fall. With each passing year I was pregnant again. This time I was still breastfeeding my second child when I became pregnant with baby number three.

With each pregnancy there was a sense of excitement and anticipation. I loved my babies. I loved having them, I loved raising them. I felt like I was in my element. It seemed like it was meant for me.

However, I found myself in a dilemma. I wasn't sure about what to do as my baby now was one hundred percent breastfed, he didn't know how to take a bottle. It was very difficult to just stop breastfeeding him, but I felt I had to in order to protect my pregnancy with my third child.

Oh, how hard it would be! My poor baby cried and cried and cried. I tried everything: spoon feeding, a baby bottle, and sippy cup. But he would have none of it. He wanted mommy's milk and that was it!

He was now a year old. I knew he was old enough to be weaned from mommy, but oh how hard it was. We had some sleepless nights to say the least.

Little Wyatt was born in January 1980. Another beautiful baby boy! He was my sweet Wyatt. Lots of dark hair and blue eyes, a beautiful combination. His smooth soft baby skin, so precious and beautiful. He had two excited little brothers who welcomed him into the family.

Mark seemed to take things in stride. His focus was more on working and, of course, drinking. He accepted each child as they came, but didn't seem to share my excitement or any other emotion for that matter, which was a part of our culture. As the years passed, life became increasingly difficult financially and in every other way.

There was just never enough money. The little he did make was gone almost before it came in. He went to his dad for a loan more than once. We came to the conclusion that we just couldn't afford our farm house, so when a house came up for rent across the road from my parents, we decided to look into selling our house. We were able to fix it up instead of paying rent.

That seemed like a great idea to us both, lifting a financial burden from our shoulders. Moving day came once again. I was not excited about this move. After all, we were moving from a nice big farm house to an old house with the siding and shingles falling off.

The house seemed dark and cold on the inside. But I had to make the best of it. My personal touches made it feel like home somewhat, but nothing could change the fact that it was a cold house in need of major repairs. It had three upstairs bedrooms and one downstairs. It had a cellar, but you couldn't really call it a basement because it didn't really have cement walls or floors. It was more like a mud floor.

This home was the beginning of the end of life as we knew it. Things were changing and it felt like a shipwreck.

Mark's drinking went from bad to worse. He wasn't just getting drunk on weekends anymore. It became almost a daily ritual. I did not understand it. How could a man with three beautiful boys and a wife be so miserable and out of touch that he felt the need to escape from the real world on a daily basis?

I wanted so badly to have our marriage healed. What could I do to make him want it too? There were times when life seemed like a nightmare I just could not wake up from.

Even though Mark got drunk on a regular basis, he never skipped work. That was one thing he did diligently. By this time, he had ten Amish men working for him and he took pride in his work.

To me it seemed like he gave it all he had, and when he came home, there was nothing left to share with us as a family. It got to the point of me dreading him coming home.

I never knew what would set him off. Anything at all could trigger his temper and we had hell to pay.

I loved living across the road from my parents. At least I had some emotional support from my mom and sisters which I needed, loved, and appreciated.

September of 1980, I got pregnant again for baby number four. Little Wyatt was only eight months old at the time. He was such a good baby. He was quiet and content, and very smart. By the time he was a year old he was tapping his feet to music and telling us his age and what month he was born.

I was hoping there was enough of me to go around being pregnant with three hungry little boys to feed. It became increasingly more difficult to accomplish. Even though we were not actually paying rent, financially we were no better off. To me it seemed there was just more money for alcohol.

We were barely getting by. If it weren't for my mom having a little grocery store and allowing me to get groceries on 'credit,' I don't know what I would've done.

We heated the house with a coal/wood burning stove and it took a lot to heat our cold, cold house. It was so cold that the kids just couldn't stay warm upstairs. There was cold air coming in everywhere. It came in through the windows and cracks in the siding. There was air coming up through the floors. It felt more like a barn than a house.

Many, many mornings when I got up it was so freezing cold that I had to put on my boots before I could go into the kitchen to make breakfast. Everything in the kitchen was frozen. We didn't have indoor plumbing or running water, so I had to carry in every drop of water I used for cooking. I had to break the ice in the water bucket before I could make coffee. Even the vanilla in my cupboard froze, breaking the glass container it was in.

It was hard to keep the boys warm. We all slept in one bedroom downstairs where the snow blew in under the bed. Oh my!

Would it ever get better? When would this end? Mark would go to work in the early morning hours, leaving me with the task of hauling in enough wood and coal to get through another day of trying to keep us from freezing. As I went out to the depleted frozen coal pile, I would pick through the fine pieces, grateful for every little chunk I could find. Even though it cut into my fingers, causing them to bleed, to me it was like black gold.

I would fire up the stove until it was red hot on the outside. Even then it would barely heat the living room. I had to close all the doors to the kitchen and bedroom so that we could stay warm. I would pull the hickory rocker as close to the hot stove as possible and hold my babies to keep them warm. Even then my feet and back would still be cold from all the cold air coming up through the cracks in the floor and through gaps around the windows. I would sit there rocking my babies with tears streaming down my cheeks.

Many times I would go spend the day at my mom's house. It was warm there. Thank God for my mother. The due date came and went for baby number four. It was April of 1981 and he was late in coming. This little guy sure was taking his time. I felt as big as a horse, each day feeling labor pains, thinking maybe he'll come today.

I planned to have him at home and have my doctor come out to deliver him. I didn't want to go to the hospital and leave my three boys behind. After all, little Wyatt was only sixteen months old and not even walking yet. And so I waited and waited and waited.

April came and went. This baby was going on the fourth week past due. Finally, early one morning around five o'clock, I was in labor full force. Mark called the doctor, but there was no way he was going to be there on time. We waited for an hour and a half.

Finally, Mark ran across the street and got my mom to come help me deliver little Alex. I felt him coming and there was no way to stop him. I was in my room all by myself when he made his appearance and so I quickly sat up and picked up baby Alex. I shook him to get him to take his first breath and he started squirming and crying, immediately he put his little fists to his mouth, looking for food.

Mark, my mom, and the doctor all walked in at the same time. I was sitting up holding the baby and the doctor said, "That's the natural thing to do, honey."

Chapter 8

What a big boy Alex was! Mom cleaned him up and put a diaper and clothes on him, then set him on the scale. He was just under ten pounds. Little Alex was a delight. He was bald. No hair at all. He was the first of my babies to be born with no hair. He had very dark brown eyes. What a handsome little hunk! He would be my mischievous one. Never a dull moment in his life.

Life was full and busy with four little boys. The last two were only sixteen months apart and little Wyatt was not walking yet. It made life pretty interesting.

The word busy did not accurately describe the way life seemed to be these days. I was twenty-two years old. At least it was May and the worst of the winter weather was gone.

The two older boys could entertain themselves pretty well, but little Wyatt felt pretty lonesome and rejected with this new baby sitting in his spot, on his mommy's lap.

Since mommy couldn't carry two babies at the same time, it caused Wyatt to start walking.

He must have thought, "Forget this, I'm walking! After all, I'm not the baby anymore."

The two older boys took it all in stride. Another addition to the family didn't faze them much. They were ever so willing to be my little helpers.

Little Sebastian who was now five years old and Caleb, who was three years old, were constant companions to each other. They also had their mischievous moments. What one didn't think of, the other one did.

These little ones made my heart full and happy. They were my life. My reason to go on. I poured my heart into them. I totally loved being a mother to them.

I was thankful for my sisters who were willing to pitch in and help me get on my feet again. There was the laundry—piles and piles of laundry—and ironing, not to mention cleaning that needed to be done and four hungry boys to feed. I always felt like there were not enough hours in a day.

I loved that my mom sent over food that could just be heated and served. I was so very thankful for the kindness, generosity, and graciousness my family bestowed upon me and fast-growing family. That is one of the many amazing traits that the Amish community has that I will always remember and cherish.

By the end of May, little Alex was three weeks old. I was feeling pretty strong, and that was a good thing, because the garden needed to be finished. I depended on the produce for many things.

I planted lots of tomatoes, onions, peppers, carrots, peas, corn, green beans, radishes, and many other vegetables which I used to can vegetable soup, hot peppers, and salsa. It was a lot of work, but it brought a sense of accomplishment, and I was always happy I did it when the cold winter days set in. There was nothing better than hot vegetable soup with bread and butter on a cold winter night.

Sebastian, Caleb, Wyatt, and Alex. Such sweet little boys! So full of life. Their inquisitive natures brought excitement and joy into our lives.

We lived a simple life, just poor people trying to make ends meet. I often wondered what life would hold for my boys. Would they make alcohol the center of life, the way we lived it? Or would they grow up to be strong, successful young men?

How I hoped and prayed the latter to be true for them. But I did not see much hope for that to happen. Didn't boys automatically gravitate to the examples they have been shown in life? And if so, there would not be much hope for them to be successful. The life they were shown was very much centered around alcoholism on a daily basis. We were barely getting by. There was hardly ever enough money for groceries, but somehow there was always plenty of alcohol.

I felt so cheated.

Was this really all that God had for me in life? What was the meaning of it all? What was my purpose on this earth? Where was I headed in life? Is this what I had to look forward to? Is this the future for me and my boys? These questions and a million more were screaming in my mind. I started reading positive self-help books and dreaming of better days ahead. Surely there was more to life. There had to be a better life, somehow, some way.

During this time, like most days, I was home with the boys when I heard a knock at the door. There stood two salesmen, going door to door selling sets of Bible story books! Wow! Really? True biblical stories written in the English language.

How I wanted to buy them. But how? I didn't even know where we stood financially. Maybe I could write a check and hope for enough money to cover it. Finally, after about an hour, the men had set up a payment plan.

I was nervous about telling Mark about the purchase. I knew he would be angry, and I was right, but I had been willing to take the verbal beating for the good of my children.

The boys loved it. I would read the stories to them, especially when I put them to bed at night. They learned how little David killed Goliath with five smooth stones and how Daniel obeyed

God and faced the lions' den fearlessly. These stories and many more helped shape the future for my boys.

I always knew there was a God somewhere out there. But how do I find him? Memories would flood my mind of the Anabaptist stories I read. The real-life stories of people being so on fire for God that they would risk their lives to study the Word and fellowship after dark in people's basements, knowing that being found out meant certain death. Yet they did it willingly.

How could I find that kind of faith? Did it still exist?

I wanted that real faith, live and abundant. I wanted to share that kind of godly love with my husband, but when I would bring it up to him, he would turn away. He was not interested and didn't want to hear any of it. He was content just following the rules in the church letter, which is not true Christianity.

This caused me to feel so alone in the world. How I longed for that spiritual and emotional connection. Why was life such a struggle? Why, why, why? A million whys and no answers. Just the same struggles over and over and over—spiritual struggles, financial struggles, emotional struggles. I kept telling myself that there was a better life ahead, a better future.

One night in particular I was so overwhelmed by the financial crisis we were in. There was no food! I needed groceries in the worst way. I asked Mark what to do. What were we going to do? He had already borrowed money from his parents, and my parents were preparing for yet another wedding which was taking place the very next day. So I couldn't ask them for money.

It was cold outside and things look bleak and hopeless. Mark came out of the barn carrying the harness to the horse.

"What are we going to do?" I asked.

"I am going to the harness shop to sell this harness for some money," he explained as he carried the harness to the waiting driver's vehicle.

Oh my goodness, has it come to this? I quickly pleaded with him to allow me to come too. I thought maybe I could get a few groceries after all. So, after selling the harness for $50, he went straight to the liquor store and bought alcohol, of course. I was lucky to be able to buy milk and bread.

Chapter 9

Wedding day arrived for my sister Tina. I was excited and happy for her and her new husband, David.

Amish weddings were a happy time in my community. There was so much scrumptious food! Weddings were days when everyone ate way too much. There was ham, fried chicken, mashed potatoes, buttered noodles, dressing, vegetables, salad, and all the delicious desserts: pies, cakes, tapioca, famous date pudding, plus homemade bread and butter.

The list of goodies was never-ending. The table waiters were kept busy serving hundreds of people. It was held at a sit-down banquet of decorated tables laden with the famous "knee patches," very thin pastries topped with sugar.

Weddings were the only place these scrumptious bounties were served in our community. Tina was a beautiful, happy bride, full of anticipation of living happily ever after. She married into a good family.

David came from a family well-respected in the community. His dad was a bishop in another district, a sister church. Mom and Dad were pleased with this new son-in-law and we were all happy for our sister.

The day after the wedding cleanup was always a big job. Many of us would go back to where the wedding took place to clean up and distribute pots, pans, dishes, and leftover foods. There was always such a huge ordeal and a lot of preparation before and after a wedding. And to think my mom and dad have five of us girls to do this for. What a big deal it was, not to mention the expense.

Our simple weddings are less expensive than our conventional weddings today because there is no cake, white dress, band, etc., but we do buy gifts for each of the cooks and servers, so this along with food and drinks is where most of the cost comes from.

Doing this for my sister's wedding brought back memories of my own wedding a few short years earlier. I was hoping that her marriage would turn out to be much happier than my own.

I began to wonder if my expectations of a married life were too high or if maybe I was falling short as a wife. Whatever the reason, it was obvious something was not right. I always imagined married life as two people being in love with each other, connecting emotionally, spiritually, physically, and caring for each other in every way, looking to each other for support. A team, as it were. I wondered if I would ever experience that kind of relationship in my marriage.

This was the way we lived our life. There were fleeting glimpses of what a happy home could be like at times when Mark wasn't drunk, when he was in a good mood and not looking for something to be angry at me for. The times when we would get together with friends or family for a cookout, just enjoying an afternoon of leisurely activities with the kids running and playing with their little cousins were happy parts of my life. The guys would do their horseshoe pitching or talk about who has the fastest horse. On days like those, all was well.

How I wished this was the norm but it was not. These short glimpses gave me hope that things could change. After all, this could not go on forever, or could it?

I was hoping that things would change, that Mark would wake up and have a desire to create a healthy relationship with his boys, to lead by example, to be the dad his little boys would be proud of.

Wasn't this every man's desire? What was I going to do if things didn't change? What could I do? I felt stuck, like I had no other option than to be who I was. An uneducated Amish woman with no transportation, no phone and no money.

STUCK!

That's the word that described my situation. Such a hopeless, overwhelmingly helpless feeling. Many times I would sit and cry. No amount of begging and pleading would change Mark's heart. He was set in his ways. He enjoyed his alcohol and he loved that buzz.

Many days and nights I would be home alone with the kids. Mark would work hard all day. He was the boss and crew leader. He had ten Amish guys working for him. He worked very hard and was proud of his workmanship and the reputation he was building among his customers. Because of this, it seemed to me like he was two different people.

During the day he was a competent crew leader but turned into someone else after work. He and the driver would either stop and buy liquor and drink on the way home, or stop off at a bar and drink until way late into the night.

It was my job to feed the kids, put them to bed, and wait and wait and wait. I'd walk the floor on pins and needles wondering if he would come home in a drunken rage or if he'd stagger off to bed. I was always on edge.

As Amish people we were not allowed to have phones or own any vehicles. We could hire a driver and we would walk to the neighbors and use their phones to call someone to take us places. I often felt hypocritical asking the neighbors to do something that was supposedly a sin for us to do.

I never understood why having a phone in your house was not allowed while getting drunk was allowed in my community.

But those were the rules.

Who was I to question them? It was best to do as I was told and just stay quiet and not voice my opinions. After all I was only a woman. And women here women were supposed to be submissive and stay quiet.

Our little neighbor didn't seem to mind me using her phone when she was available, and I really appreciated her for that. I couldn't go to her house before noon since she was not an early riser. And that meant the line was usually busy.

Back then there were no private lines. Everyone shared the phone lines and sometimes it was busy for an hour or more with people catching up on all the latest gossip and you could hear every word that they said.

"Oh," I thought to myself, "if only I had my own phone." There were so many "if only's."

If only I had an education, if only I would be more self-sufficient, if only I hadn't gotten married so young.

If only my husband loved me as much as he loves his alcohol.

If only he was the husband at night as he was in the daytime— sober, hard-working, kind, considerate, kindly pleasing his customers. I believe he would've been that kind of husband and dad if the alcohol addiction wasn't in control in his life.

If only, if only.

Chapter 10

One kind old gentleman that worked for Mark was a pleasant old man. At one time he was a preacher and had walked away from the pulpit because his wife divorced him and took everything he had. His name was Simon and he lived in Dunkirk with his mother.

It seemed like he was always at our house. He didn't have much left to live for, in his opinion, so he took Mark and his crew to work each day and drank with him at night. Even on weekends Mark would have him come over just in case he needed to do some errands to run or jobs to look at, which was usually the case.

This went on for a long time until Simon's mom died. We didn't see much of him after that happened. I always felt sorry for him and hoped he would find peace and happiness. So much heartbreak. Were there any happy marriages anywhere?

It was a typical Sunday afternoon. We had been invited to my brother's house for lunch along with some more family and friends. We put the boys into the back of the buggy and drove the mile and a half to my brother's house where the people had already started to gather. The men were in the barn, the women were preparing the meal and the children were playing outside. Just a typical Sunday get together.

We women prepared the lunch as we visited and talked about all that had happened since we last saw each other. We talked about planting our gardens and all the canning we hoped to do. We talked about our accomplishments for the week. And of course, our latest pregnancies. There was always one of us pregnant, and this time it was me.

We didn't talk much about our hopes and dreams. There didn't seem to be much of that amongst us Amish women. Our conversations were centered around our kids, husbands, things that were going on in the community, where the next church was being held, or the next quilting taking place. Many times, we would confide in each other and talk about the struggles, pain and frustrations of the alcohol abuse as it seemed to get increasingly worse.

Overall, it was a pleasant, fun-filled day. The kids enjoyed playing with their cousins.

Seven-year-old Sebastian, five-year-old Caleb, three-year-old Wyatt and two-year-old Alex all had cousins close to their age. They played well and seemed to enjoy each other as they played "horse," tag, or hide and seek. It gave me a break momentarily, which I was happy for, since I was pregnant in my first trimester and tired all the time.

Our day of visiting came to a close and everyone was getting ready to go home. The men hitched the horses to their buggies, and all the kids said their good byes, we headed for home.

After a day of drinking hard liquor, things would usually escalate out of control. This day was no different and ended up to be especially violent to the point that I was afraid and could not go on. It was like I hit a brick wall. I could not do this anymore.

After Mark left again in the horse and buggy, taking our oldest son with him, I was afraid for his safety. I knew there was nothing I could do. I got the rest of the boys settled the best I could, assuring them that all will be ok. My mom heard the commotion and came to our aid.

I said, "Mom, I have to leave."

She said, "I understand. I'll keep the kids for as long as it takes you."

And so she took the boys home with her.

I went out behind the house and cried out to God, begging and pleading with him to get me out of this mess. I didn't know if he would hear my cries. I knew I had to leave. But where? I had no phone, no money and no transportation. I was so stuck! I felt like I had no choice but to walk to my little neighbor's house and call someone. But who? It was Sunday evening. Who could I call? Where could I go? I didn't have a clue.

As I walked over to my little old neighbor's house to use the phone, I had no idea who to call or where to go if I did reach someone, or even what I was going to tell them.

Who would want any part of this mess? But I was compelled. I was driven to keep going. I put one foot in front of the other and finally I reached the door of my dear neighbor's house.

I was greatly relieved that she answered the door and knew who to call. I was at a loss as to who I could reach on a Sunday evening to come pick me up. Even if they did, where would I go?

As I reached for the receiver on the black rotary phone, I dialed the phone number of a distant cousin. I thought maybe I could stay with her for a couple days to think things through, but no answer.

So I thought of Simon, the elderly man who had at one time worked for Mark, but I had no way of knowing where to find him.

Finally, I dialed zero for the operator and asked for his last name in Dunkirk, and she gave me the number of Simon's ex-wife. I felt that I had no other options but to dial her number. Maybe she could at least tell me where to find him. So I dialed the number, and lo and behold, Simon answered the phone. I could not believe my ears.

I asked Simon if he could please pick me up. I told him what had happened.

He turned to his ex-wife and told her what was going on. He said, "I know what she's going through. I'm going after her." He had worked for my husband and saw the abuse first hand, so he knew what I was going through.

So he and his ex-wife came and picked me up.

Simon said when they arrived, "We will take you to my sister's house. She is a Christian. She may be able to help you."

I breathed a sigh of relief. For tonight, at least I would be safe and I could think. My oldest son was still with his dad, and I was so worried about him, but at least the other three were safe with my mom.

Maybe, just maybe, there was help out there somewhere.

I was a little apprehensive about meeting Simon's sister. Her name was Martha; she was widowed and lived alone.

We reached Martha's house. By this time, it was getting dark. I was exhausted and I had a splitting headache, still worried about my oldest son.

Martha was a sweet gray-haired woman a little taller than myself. She seemed like an angel to me. So kind, loving, compassionate, and understanding. She welcomed me into her home with open arms and began telling me about the wonderful love and grace of God.

She talked about the Word of God and what he did for us on the cross. I had heard that before, but when she told me the story in detail it became so clear to me. It became alive!

Martha gave me many, many scriptures—promises of God. She told me how much God loved me, that he is my Heavenly Father, Jesus the son of God who shed his blood and became sin for me. He conquered death and hell so that I could live a victorious life of freedom in him. I didn't have to live a beaten down life in bondage to sin and strife.

He tells us in both the old and New Testament to LOVE Him with all of our heart, mind, and soul. (Deuteronomy 6:5 and Mark 12:30 KJV) He tells us in 1st Corinthians 13:2 that if we don't have love, we have absolutely nothing. Love is a very strong, powerful force and we must be deeply rooted in it. Without love we are ineffective. Without love we cannot enter into His gates. We must love Him above all else before we can love our neighbor, and we must love our neighbor as ourselves.

How can we take that first step if our love tank is depleted? How can we love God if we don't know Him? Even more importantly, how can we know Him? Do we get to know Him on a personal level by going to church? If so, which one?

That is one huge question in today's world where churches have lost their first love, have built fences, and have become cold and judgmental. The answer is found in the Word of God. We must know the Word of God. That is how we get to know Him. By praying and reading His Word. Having fellowship with like-minded people.

By asking God to fill you with His Holy Spirit. Believe me, He wants it for us more than we want it for ourselves. Jude 1:20 tells us to build each other up in our most Holy Faith and pray in the power of the Holy Spirit. We must be deeply rooted! She said he is such a loving God and that he also loves my husband.

I was taken aback. I couldn't believe that what she was saying was true.

How could it be? How could a holy God love a mean, angry drunk? How was that even possible? I know I sure didn't like him when he was drunk. He was unbearable to live with.

I wanted so much to believe what Martha was telling me was true. My Amish sect had always taught that the way into heaven was obeying the church letter and with good works. Could it really be possible that God was as kind, compassionate, and loving as this sweet lady was telling me? After all, she read it to me from her English Bible.

Did my German Bible say the same thing? Was it possible that my sins could be forgiven? Can a holy God truly love me? I felt unlovable, like a piece of trash at the bottom of the barrel. I felt I was not worthy of such love. And it was free?

Why hadn't I heard it before? Here I was, twenty-four years old, and had never known that kind of love.

I wanted to believe it. I so much wanted it to be true.

Chapter 11

It was late. My head was hurting.

I asked Martha, "Do you have anything for a headache?"

She answered, "All I have for headaches is Jesus!"

Wow! Total dependence on Jesus for everything? I'd never heard that before. But I was intrigued. That was the kind of faith I wanted to have. It reminded me of the stories I read as a young girl about the Anabaptist people who literally lived every minute for Christ, even unto death.

I didn't realize there were actually people in this day and age that had that kind of faith. It gave me a glimmer of hope. I went to bed at Martha's house that night feeling hopeful and encouraged. I had to find that kind of faith no matter the cost. I hoped my German Bible would tell this is true.

I woke up the next morning to a whole new world. Everything seemed like it was going to be okay. It was like a black cloud had lifted, like a bright warm sunshine after the storm.

I felt love like I'd never felt before. I wanted more of that precious word Martha told me about, those amazing promises. I just had to find out if my German Bible had those same promises.

Faith is a living hope. Grace is a free gift. I had to accept it in order for it to be mine. A free gift is a gift, but only if the receiver accepts it.

1 Corinthians 13:13 says, "And now faith, hope, love, these three; but the greatest of these is love." (KJV) And I wanted to experience that kind of love.

Simon came back and picked me up from Martha's house, not sure where to take me to in order for me to be protected. He said I could stay in his trailer. It was vacant since he was back with his ex-wife, and so I agreed, although the stay was short-lived.

Simon came to tell me Mark had called and told him to bring me home if he knew what was good for him. And so, of course, that is what he did.

My husband had kept my oldest son out all night. Physically, he was fine, but he had probably been hurt emotionally.

But I had no fear! I felt like I was in a whole new world. There was nothing too hard for me. I could do all things through Christ who strengthens me. I learned later that this promise literally becomes my lifeline.

God is so good! Peace, sweet peace. Amazing love! I cannot describe the unbelievable love, peace, and joy I felt after my stay with Martha and reading the amazing promises of God, the Great and Mighty King of the universe, the one who spoke the stars into existence. The Awesome One. How can he love someone such as me? The unworthy, unloveable piece of nothing that I am.

He died for me? A wretched sinner am I. And my sins are washed away? Oh, what glory. He conquered death, hell and the grave. How glorious! How amazing! Peace, peace, sweet peace. What a difference, what a transformation a day makes.

I was happy to get back home. Mom took great care of all my boys. My little Sebastian came home safely. Thank you, Lord Jesus! Mark, my husband seemed to have mixed feelings about my return. Should he be happy or should I be punished? After all, to him I was his piece of property and had no right to be happy unless he chose me to be.

He kept looking at me in a strange way, trying to figure out what happened to me or why I could possibly be peaceful and happy. It seemed to me like he was trying to figure his next course of action. Should he be angry with me or happy that I'm home? Leaving home without permission is not something we did as Amish women and I wasn't sure what to expect.

I couldn't wait for the next day when Mark would go back to work so that I could take the horse and buggy and drive into town to purchase an English Bible. I just had to find out for myself if all those wonderful life-giving scriptures could be found in my German Bible.

I couldn't wait to tell my mom of my wonderful transformation and let her know how amazing our Heavenly Father really is. Surely, if I can show it to her in scripture, she would be delighted to accept it as I had done. All these thoughts and more raced through my mind as I listened to the clip-clopping of the horse's hooves on the pavement and the noise of the steel-rimmed buggy wheels on the road. I slowly made my way to the Faith and Life Bookstore where I found what I was looking for—an English Bible, King James Version. And thus, my search began.

Peace, sweet peace, oh so wonderful. His living Word was coming alive to me more and more with each passing day. I loved saturating myself in His Word and in His Presence. It became my oasis of safety, peace, serenity, and love like I had never experienced before. Such love! Sweet unconditional love.

This was so different than what I'd been taught my whole life. I didn't have to do anything to earn salvation. I just had to accept it and believe it. Jesus paid such a horrendous price for me so that I might live. He bled and died for me. He was beaten beyond recognition and did so willing for my sins. I cannot even begin to comprehend what he went through for me. To pay for my sins, He who knew no sin took my heavy burden upon himself and conquered death, hell and the grave and gave me sweet victory.

How could I be so arrogant to think I could add to what he had already done? Never could I ever do anything to merit eternal life. He did it already. All I could do was say, "Thank you, Lord," and love Him with all my heart, mind, and soul.

As my new-found excitement began to grow and my walk with the Lord became more and more dear to my heart, I just had to share it with my mom.

I said to her, "Mom, the Lord is so real to me. He gives me such peace."

And she reminded me that we must follow the teachings of our forefathers and that we should not question their teachings. She reminded me that I promised to stay true to God and His church. She said, "We can't esteem ourselves better than our wise forefathers."

This brought such confusion to my mind. Who are our forefathers? Don't we go all the way back to Abraham, Isaac, and Jacob? Are they not our forefathers? Do I not have a right to question my faith and research the Word of God?

Does the Bible not tell us to study to show ourselves approved? Did I not promise God to stay true to Him? Does this not mean I should follow Him and allow Him to lead me?

All these questions so many more went through my mind. I knew I had to follow Him and not man, no matter the cost. After all, this is about my eternal destiny.

I love and respected my mom, but the Word says that he that is not willing to forsake all to follow Him is not worthy. And I just knew that no matter where the Lord would lead me, I would follow.

Ralph and Avis were our new neighbors. They bought the house where our sweet neighbor had lived. Her son had sold the house after she'd passed.

We became close friends very quickly. Not only did they allow me to use their phone, but they also offered to take me where I needed to go. They were a kind, loving couple. They were both Native American Indian but looked quite opposite of each other. Ralph was tall with blond hair and blue eyes. Avis was shorter with black hair and very dark eyes. Ralph explained to us that he was from a tribe of Indians with blue eyes and blond hair.

I longed for the loving relationship with my husband like they had with each other.

Chapter 12

The times we spent with Ralph and Avis during family outings became very enjoyable as well as memorable. They took us and our boys to an Indian wedding. This was all new to us and very fascinating, quite the eye opener for me.

The wedding was fun—lots of music, drums, chanting, and dancing. The ceremony consisted of the bride and groom exchanging vows, but instead of exchanging rings, they wrapped a shawl or blanket around them both. It was very interesting.

Ralph and Avis loved their Indian heritage and taught us a lot about it. They enjoyed cooking Indian food for us and took us to their pow-wows. Watching them dance was one of my favorite things about the event. I began to look forward to our visits with Ralph and Avis.

They soon saw how Amish women were treated and on occasion brought it to my attention. They wanted me to know that isn't normal, that women should be treated equally to men, and that I shouldn't have to endure the abusive situation I was living in.

Ralph would ask Mark, "Do you love your wife?"

Mark would reply with a smirk, "Well I married her, didn't I?"

That was always his answer. I'd heard it a thousand times. Some of his drinking buddies or his drivers would ask him that very question he would give the same answer.

He would also add, "She's lucky to have me," making me feel like a piece of garbage that was lucky to have a trash can to live in.

Life no longer seemed unbearable, not since Christ came into my life. I now had a sense of purpose. Life was worth living.

I wish I could say having Christ in my life caused all the chaos, confusion, abuse, and painful times disappear but that is not the case. What it did do is help me cope with it all. I now had someone to turn to. I was hopeful that things would change. I was hoping for a change of heart in my husband. If only he could experience the love of God, his mercy and forgiveness—that would change everything. What a dream come true that would be! A family united as one in Christ where we all loved the Lord according to Mark 12:30. I hoped and prayed.

We continued to go to church occasionally. My husband was never excited about going, even though it was only twice a month, as Amish traditionally have church every other Sunday. And when he didn't go, I didn't go either. Amish women very seldom go alone, especially a woman like me who had four boys and another on the way.

But that didn't stop me from growing in the Lord. I loved my Lord. Not a day went by that He didn't do something special in my life and allowed me to feel His peace and presence. That feeling is indescribable. Such assurance I've never known.

My husband continued drinking. Things weren't any better, and if anything it got worse. Every night was an ordeal. Any little thing would set him off. Dinner time was especially trying times for us. Trying to get through dinner with four boys was getting to be too much for all of us. It was not a pleasant time, not like it was when I was a kid at home. When I was growing up, we would all sit at the dinner table and eat the meal together, enjoying each other's company. It was a pleasant time.

Why could it not be like that for us? It was so hard to get through. In fact, it got to the point where I would feed the kids before my husband got home from work. The less interaction with him, the better.

It seemed like we hardly ever got to spend any quality time together as a family. The devastations of an alcoholic home— the hurts, the disappointments, the broken promises took their toll.

Lord, when would all this ever stop? Or would it never stop?

Somehow, some way things, just had to get better. Somehow I knew they would. Somehow I felt like there was a better life ahead.

I started to pray that God would make my husband so sick of the alcohol that he would quit drinking. Surely, if he just had a taste of the living water, he wouldn't want the alcohol anymore. So I prayed and prayed and fasted and prayed until one day Mark became sick.

He was sick to the point that he was worried he wasn't going to make it. One day after another, he lay sick in bed. He asked me to pray for him. I asked if I could read the Word of God to him which he agreed to.

I told him of God's all-powerful love and forgiveness, and how much God loved him and wanted to deliver him from the alcoholism. I told him about the peace of living a surrendered life to Christ, how sweet it would be.

This was a turning point. Mark agreed to invite the Lord Jesus into his heart and asked for forgiveness. He was ready to surrender the alcohol if God would heal him and help him through this sickness. And He did!

He got better and stopped drinking.

I was ecstatic! Wow! How great is my God? This is an absolute miracle! My husband and I would serve God together. How wonderful that would be. Raising our boys together in the Lord. Is that not every Amish mama's dream?

Life was getting better by the day. My husband was being a dad to the kids. He was no longer a grouchy drunk when he got home from work. He helped me with the boys and we started doing things together. Even his countenance changed. We were serving a God of miracles.

There was hope! I was excited and encouraged. I wanted to shout it from the housetops.

Hallelujah!

Chapter 13

My husband continued to work hard. He was always busy doing something. If he wasn't on a job working alongside his ten employees, he was out with a potential customer pricing jobs and giving quotes. Many times on these occasions he would take me and the boys with him just so we could spend more time together. Times like this gave me great hope that my dreams of a happy loving home were finally coming true.

However, I soon realized this happiness was short lived as Mark started working for a man that described his new found peace in Christ, he said he too was a born again Christian and could relate to the peace and happiness.

And then he told Mark, "You know, it is not wrong to drink!"

He showed Mark in the bible where Jesus turned water into wine. I was so devastated when Mark went back to his old drinking habits, dashing my hopes and dreams to a million broken pieces.

Oh dear Lord! Surely this nightmare is not starting all over again! Just when it seemed like happiness was just within reach. How in the world would I be able to go through it again?

Somehow I had to believe my Heavenly Father was still in control. I had to believe that. I had to stay strong in my faith in him. He was my only hope. Somehow he would see us through.

After my hopes and dreams of being a Christian couple and loving the Lord together were dashed to a million pieces, I wasn't sure which way to turn. I prayed, "Lord, where do I go from here? One minute I am excited beyond words to have my husband surrender his heart to Christ and the next day he's back on the bottle throwing everything to the wind. Really? Can this really happen?"

I couldn't even imagine throwing away the love I felt for my Lord and Savior. And for what? For alcohol? Oh, dear Lord, have mercy on his soul. I just knew I was going to serve my Lord no matter what! If I have to serve Him alone, I was willing.

As I continued my walk with Christ alone, searching for more truth, growing in the Lord, visiting churches, I sensed that God was leading me out of the Amish church. I knew what that meant and I did not want to leave. How could I? This was my whole world! It was my life, my love, my security, all that was near and dear to my heart. I knew nothing about the world outside of my Amish community and I was not interested in trying to leave my world.

So I stayed.

I told myself, "I can stay here and still serve God."

Or so I thought.

But the more I went to the Amish church and listened to the sermons, the more my heart was grieved within me. I couldn't hide the tears as I sat in church and listened to them preach about my Jesus as if He was a storybook character, like you couldn't have a personal relationship with him.

I wanted to get up and tell them, "He is real, He is alive!" I wanted to ask them if they really knew who Jesus is. He is not a figment of the imagination. He died for you and me. He went through tremendous pain, anguish and rejection so that we might be saved. Oh, Lord, have mercy on us!

The more I questioned the Amish religion, and the more I studied, it became very clear to me that the Amish religion was started by mere man, specifically by Jakob Ammann. It started within a group of Swiss and Alsatian Anabaptists in 1693. Those who followed Ammann became known as Amish. And then in the second half of the 19th century, the Amish divided into Old Order Amish and Amish Mennonites.

There was nowhere in the German Bible, the English Bible or any other version of the Bible that said I had to be Amish or wear Amish clothes in order to go to heaven. It was another denomination with rules made up by man. Not God.

I realized this was not going to get me into heaven. The only way into heaven is through Jesus Christ and Him alone. This is true according to the written word of God. John 14:6 says, "I am the way, the truth, and the life; no one comes to the Father, but by me." (KJV)

I knew I had a big decision to make. It was too big for me to make alone. Wasn't the husband supposed to be making these kinds of decisions? God did not create the woman to carry this responsibility alone. He made woman as a helpmeet for the man, and together they were to make these huge, life-changing decisions.

This was not just about me, or him, it was about our children as well. I would try to talk to him about these things but he wouldn't hear any of it. He wanted to stay within his comfort zone and drink. He was not interested in anything that required change.

Sebastian was six years old. It was time to enroll him into school. But where were we going to send him to? The Amish Parochial School or the Public School in town? Another decision to make.

Amish children in my sect were allowed to go to public school. I knew I wanted him to receive the best education in order for him to grow up and make healthy decisions in life. I wanted so much more for him than I had achieved in life for myself. I did not want him to be uneducated and stuck like me. I did not want my boys to grow up believing that the life of alcoholism is the norm.

I prayed, "Oh, dear God, lead, guide and direct my boys. Help them to make healthy choices in life."

I decided to visit the local public school and enrolled our son. This was the very first time I ever set foot inside a public-school building and it was overwhelming! It was so big! So many rooms, so many hallways. So much different from the one-room Amish school that I grew up in. Would my little boy survive this big world? Is this too much for him?

No. I decided the pattern had to be broken. I had to take the chance and allow my son to do this if he was going to make more of himself than he would being raised up going to the Amish school.

Chapter 14

The first day of school came all too soon. That big yellow bus seemed intimidating as I watched my little boy hop on board. He didn't seem as apprehensive as I felt. I prayed for God to be with him, I prayed he would like his teacher. I hoped he would have friends that would help him adjust in this new adventure in his young life. I couldn't wait for him to tell me all about it.

I was waiting for him when he came home that night and was relieved that he seemed to enjoy his first day. He had a great teacher and he couldn't say enough about how nice and kind she was to him.

Thank you, Lord. Just maybe his would work. I sure hoped so.

Monday morning came and along with it came the challenges of life. Sebastian had already gotten on the bus when Mark's driver still hadn't shown up to take him to work. This was a constant problem, finding a good driver with a dependable vehicle. It was getting to be a huge problem. A day of missed work turned into a consistent pattern. This meant less of a pay check not only for Mark, but his ten employees as well.

One day Mark had had enough of the non-dependable drivers and decided to go against the rules of the church. He bought his own vehicle, a big twelve-passenger van. It would stay parked at our house and he would hire an extra non-Amish employee so that he would always have a way to go to work. This was a temporary solution and momentary relief. He would deal with the consequences later.

About this same time I had been visiting with our English neighbors on a regular basis. The neighbors lived around the corner from us and we all got along with each other. They would have us over for cookouts and our children played well with each other. It was the first time my boys were introduced to Nintendo and soon fell in love with Pac-Man. They played and played for hours on end.

One day my neighbor Judy offered to take me to get my driver's permit. What a frightening thought! What would happen if I did that? The church would certainly have me reprimanded for it, and what would Mark say? What would he do? I couldn't see how things could much worse since he hadn't been taking us to any church as of late—not to the Amish church, not to any church.

So hesitantly, I agreed to go get my permit. Judy took me in her car as her husband Ed watched my boys. I told her it was very important that I get back before Mark got home from work or there would be consequences to pay.

What a mix of emotions! I was excited, apprehensive, and frightened all at the same time, but hopeful too that maybe, just maybe, there's a brighter future ahead. I would keep this little secret of having my driver's permit to myself for now. No one needed to know. After all, I didn't know if I'd even get my driver's license. It's not like I had anything to worry about. What Mark and the church didn't know wouldn't hurt them or me. At least not today.

I got home just in time to greet Sebastian as he came home from school. I started dinner as he told me all about his day. He loved his teacher but learning didn't come easy for him. He struggled to keep his mind focused on his work.

He had made friends with other Amish kids at school which was a relief to me. It made the adjustment a little easier, and even though his Amish friends were from another district, it didn't seem to interfere with their friendship. It was hard to keep the driver's permit secret to myself, but I knew it had to be that way for now.

Maybe the time would come when I could talk to Mark about it, but just not now. Besides, when would I tell him? He was drunk every night. And the only time I saw him half-sober was in the mornings which was only for a short time since he left for work early, before daylight. And I couldn't possibly discuss such a huge issue like getting my driver's permit without his permission. He might just go and tell the bishop.

Moses and Martha were some friends of ours who lived only a few miles from us. They dressed somewhat similar to our Amish dress. The church they belonged to was called The Assembly. They lived more modern than us. They had the modern conveniences and drove cars, but did not believe in having a television in the house. They offered to pick me up and take me to church with them, and I occasionally accepted their invitation, and found it to be a very pleasant experience. I was introduced to a whole new group of people who understood the born again experience I'd had. This was very comforting and reassuring.

I quickly became friends with Alice who was married to one of the ministers of The Assembly. She knew I had a lot of questions and invited me to come to her house and talk with her and her husband when he came home for lunch. She said Ken would be happy to answer my questions.

This was a huge ordeal as I had to hitch up the horse and buggy to drive into town, which meant I needed to ask my mom to keep the boys for hours and still try to be home before Mark came home from work. I knew it would be tough to do, but I was willing to do just about anything to get some answers. I just had to know the truth about the Word.

It was not easy to find a place to tie my horse to in the parking lot of the apartment complex, but finally decided to use the dumpster to tie her up.

As I made my way to her apartment, Alice greeted me at the door and made me feel welcome. She showed me into the living room and proceeded into the kitchen to finish preparing lunch for her husband Ken. And so I waited patiently in the living room. Alice brought me a glass of water, and we made small talk until her husband Ken came home.

He walked straight into the kitchen where he washed his hands, quietly ate his lunch, never saying a word to me or even acknowledging my presence. He spoke very little with his wife Alice, finished eating his lunch, and left to go back to work.

Wow! I was taken aback! Is this what Christian ministers are all about? I did not know what to make of all this. It seemed to me that Alice felt awkward when her husband left the house to go back to work without speaking to me.

She said, "I will introduce you to my neighbor. I see her out in her yard shelling peas. Her name is Sharon and she believes a lot like we do. Maybe she could answer some of your questions and give you a better understanding of the Word."

And so she introduced me to her neighbor. There was an immediate connection between Sharon and myself. I loved her immediately. What I loved most was that she knew a lot about scripture, and everything she told me she backed up by the Word. That was very reassuring.

I had just found my new best friend. We talked and talked. I stayed as long as I dared to and then hurried home as fast as my horse would take me. I was excited and hopeful, and if this visit would get me in trouble, it was totally worth it.

Chapter 15

I was so encouraged to have found a friend who was willing to help me. I looked forward to the days I could make the ten-mile trip into town with the horse and buggy.

Sharon had her pastor and his wife meet me at the park where we talked and fellowshipped around the things of God. They answered questions and gave me more information than I knew what to do with. I was ecstatic.

I now understood the kind of faith The Anabaptist people gave their lives for. A living hope. A reassurance of knowing that earthly death means eternal salvation. A home in heaven beyond our comprehension.

It was a very hot summer. I was very pregnant! It was time for baby number five to make his appearance. We were going to have my aunt deliver my baby since she was a midwife. I went to her house for a check-up, since I had been having labor pains. I explained that I was extremely exhausted since it was so hot and we had no fans and no air conditioning. It was a very hot July in Indiana and I could not sleep.

In the middle of the night I would stick my head out of the door just to be able to breathe. I was miserable. Night after night I got very little sleep. And my aunt gave me herbs to take and castor oil to drink. She came out to the house and stayed for hours when I was in labor. She and my husband Mark helped me push and push and push.

And finally, my beautiful angel face baby number five made his appearance. Oh, dear Lord, what an ordeal. This was by far the toughest delivery I'd ever had. Another boy. Five boys! He was so beautiful. It was a huge relief to have this over with.

He had a perfect little face. He looked like an angel. But what would we name him? I had all girl names picked out because I was sure he was going to be a girl. Everything was different about the pregnancy. I'd carried him higher. According to his heart rate and everything I was convinced he would be a girl.

The day came when I got brave enough to invite Sharon out to our home and meet Mark and the boys. She was willing to come, knowing she may or may not be accepted by my husband. I was apprehensive since I didn't know if he would be drunk or sober. It just so happened that Mark's dad was there too and so she got to witness to him along with my husband.

I was pleased that no one got angry with me for doing this, but at the same time, Mark kept a tighter rein on me and watched every move I made. He even forbade me to call Sharon anymore since her influence was leading me in a direction he didn't want to go.

By this time, I had told Mark about having my driver's permit, and so he took it upon himself to go to the Amish preachers and tell them about his rebellious wife having a driver's permit and talking to Englishers about scripture. These things were strictly forbidden.

Even more of a sin than getting drunk.

How backwards! I felt like everything was closing in on me and pretty much felt like I was living with the enemy. He wouldn't allow me to communicate with anyone outside of our circle of friends and family. Every night when he came home, I had to give an account of my whole day. Where had I been to? Who had I spoken with?

God was watching over me. He was always right there. Leading me, guiding me. It seemed like every time I needed Sharon to talk to, I'd run into her at the grocery or the laundromat, this one time in particular I was so badly needing to talk to her. I was forbidden to call her, so while I was at the laundromat doing laundry, I kept praying and telling the Lord that I wasn't allowed to call Sharon, but that He could have Sharon call the phone at the laundromat.

I even stood by the phone on the wall, hoping that it would ring. The phone didn't ring and I went back home.

The next time I saw Sharon, she asked, "What were you doing on Tuesday?"

I answered, "I was doing my laundry at the laundromat."

She gasped and said, "The Lord kept telling me, 'Call Eirene, call Eirene' and I said, 'Lord, she doesn't have a phone!' Next time I'll call the laundromat."

Oh, what a mighty God we serve. He is so faithful. I took every opportunity I could to go to meetings at the park with Sharon and her pastor and his wife, sometimes taking my boys with me. This was the highlight of the week for me. By this time, I was convinced that I was to leave the church and follow Him.

He told me in his word, "He who loves father and mother more than me is not worthy of me; and he that loveth son or daughter more than me is not worthy of me." -Matthew 10:37 (KJV).

As I grew in the Lord and matured spiritually, the gap or wall between my husband and I seemed to get bigger and bigger. He did not share my love and appreciation for the Word of God. If anything, he just drowned himself more and more with alcohol and seemed out of touch with reality.

I began to wonder if this divided way of living was to be my lot in life. It seemed we had very little in common anymore. We still lived in the same house, slept in the same bed, but never ate our meals together, and we never ever ate meals together as a family anymore.

I was certain this was not the way God intended for us to live. This is not the way a healthy family was supposed to live. How was I to ever leave all this to follow Him?

As Sharon and I grew closer, we confided in and encouraged each other and prayed for a breakthrough for Mark. We prayed God would open his heart and cause him to be willing to talk to her pastor. I knew that would be a miracle, and he did finally agree to allow the pastor to come to the house to listen to him—reluctantly, of course. It was later in the day.

Sharon came over along with pastor Tom, his daughter, and son-in-law. Mark came home soon after they got there, but instead of coming in and greeting them, he made an excuse to escape to the barn where he started drinking whiskey. He refused to come in. They sat and waited very patiently. After what seemed like hours, we concluded that Mark decided not to join us after all and so pastor Tom decided to pray.

We were all kneeling together and praying, and it was dark outside by this time. All of a sudden there was a loud bang and shattering glass. A flashlight flew through the air, barely missing the pastor's head as he ducked. Mark threw the flashlight with the intention of hitting pastor Tom.

Needless to say, they hurried out of there. Before leaving, they asked me if I wanted to leave with them, but I stayed.

I was mortified.

Oh, dear God! What was I to do? How was I ever going to follow Christ with this abusive alcoholic who was clearly controlled by demonic forces. I just did not know where to turn or what to do.

My poor, bewildered little boys. What must they be thinking or feeling? I knew that none of this made any sense to them. Dear Lord, help us.

As soon as I could, I called Sharon from my neighbor's phone. I told her it was impossible for me to leave, and so we agreed in prayer that if it really was God's will for us to leave, then He would have to make it happen. I couldn't do it. He had to make it happen one way or another, and so for the next couple weeks, we prayed.

I prayed, "Lord, I am willing to follow you. I am willing to serve you but I cannot do it alone. It will take a miracle."

And I left it there. It was all up to Him.

Chapter 16

Weeks passed. It was in the cold of winter. Mark and his dad were outside drinking when they had the bright idea to take his dad home in the van Mark bought. He had no driver's license and knew how illegal this was. Neither him nor his dad were in their right minds, so there was no convincing them not to do this. They had their minds made up.

To this day we don't know who turned Mark in for driving drunk without a license, but someone did. As he pulled into our driveway, the police pulled in behind him. He got out of the van. The police gave him the sobriety test, which he failed miserably.

After the policeman had me take the boys inside the house, they cuffed Mark and sat him in the back of their cruiser. I was bewildered. This was all new to me. I didn't know what to do. They couldn't take my husband away from me—I had five little boys. I needed my husband to stay and help me.

As the policeman were about to pull out of the driveway with my husband, I hurried out to the car and asked them, "When is he coming back?"

The officer gave me a funny look and said, "Ma'am, if he's not back in fifteen minutes, he's not coming back."

I was devastated to say the least. What was I going to do? Where would I go? What would happen next? My mind was racing. My stomach was in knots. My husband was in jail. Oh, dear Lord. What now?

All I could do was get on my knees and pray. My Heavenly Father was my only hope. He was the only source of security I had. Oh, how I needed Him now. I tried to comfort my boys the best I could. How do I explain all of this to them? None of it would make any sense.

I prayed with them and did my best to comfort them and ease their anxious hearts. Oh, dear God. This all needed to stop. I just couldn't go on living this chaotic life of confusion and pain, such an emotional roller coaster.

I prayed, "Show me, Lord, what you would have me to do. Lead, guide and direct me." After praying and lamenting I fell into a fitful sleep.

I contacted our friend Moses who went out to tell Mark's dad what had happened, and together they went and bailed Mark out of jail. He came home knowing he was in deep trouble. He had a judge to face in court. Where was the money coming from to pay fines and court costs? It was dead of winter. We were living in a cold house where I had to break the ice in the water bucket before I could make our morning coffee. I shared a kitchen with a host of mice who made their appearance on top of my cabinets.

"Dear God," I cried. "How? Where? When?"

I felt so, so very hopeless and helpless. I did not sign up for this. I did not realize it at the time, but all this pain and chaos was God working in His mysterious ways.

The very next church Sunday after Mark went to Jail, Bishop Dave paid us a visit on his way to church. He came in with his familiar, friendly smile. After some small talk and pleasantries, he asked Mark if it was true that he had spent the night in jail.

Mark answered, "Yes, it's true."

Bishop Dave then asked if we had planned on attending service that day.

Mark said, "No, probably not today."

And so bishop Dave said, "You guys come on over for barbecued chicken sometime." And he turned and left.

He went straight to church and excommunicated both Mark and myself.

This was a huge pivotal point in our life. Since we had been excommunicated, Mark lost all of his Amish employees just like that. They could no longer work for him because now they had to shun him.

How devastating! Our income, Mark's livelihood, was stripped from him. Our whole world was turned upside down, all because Mark spent the night in jail.

I had to call Sharon and share the news with her that we had been excommunicated from the Amish church. This was, to me, God's way of getting us out of the Amish church.

I could have never dreamed this up. I wouldn't have chosen it to be this way. Nevertheless, not my will, Lord, but yours be done. I didn't have to do anything. I prayed and put it all in God's hands.

Truly, Romans 8:28 is true, true for me and my family. It tells me that all things work together for good to those who love the Lord and are called according to His purpose. God is so good! He is so faithful and loving and merciful. How good God is! He is amazing! I was sad about leaving my world behind, but grateful that He deems me worthy to suffer for His sake.

After being excommunicated from the Amish church, everything changed. Our whole world was turned upside down and inside out. I cannot even describe the mix of emotions.

It was worse than a funeral because we lost contact with all of our Amish family, friends, acquaintances, leaving all that we'd ever known to venture out into unknown territory by blind faith.

If Mark would have repented, they would have ended the shunning, but he didn't. Not only was Mark shunned—I was too along with our kids. I trusted that my God was leading me, walking with me, even carrying me in this huge life-changing decision.

If we had ever hit bottom, it was now. How I wished that my husband and I could be on the same page spiritually. It would've made this transition so much easier. My sisters came over to talk to me, pleading with me to reconsider my decision to leave the church. My heart went out to them. I so much wanted them to understand that I had to do this. I had to follow Him. It hurt me to see them hurt. These girls were in my heart. We were sisters, we were family, blood relatives. The last thing I wanted to do is hurt them.

I tried to explain to them that this is what I needed to do to obey my Lord. I said, "I am not doing this to hurt you, that is the last thing I want to do. I don't want to leave you. I am only going to a different church, I am not turning away from God."

But it seemed they could not understand.

Why was this so hard? Why did it have to be this way? Isn't there such a thing as respect for each other's spiritual decisions? It wasn't like I wanted to go out and be crazy. I simply desired to obey my Savior. That simple.

We had to remove ourselves from the community. Mark had lost his whole crew. We had absolutely nothing. We felt paralyzed with fear and uncertainty.

What do you do when lose all you've ever known? I felt many emotions. I felt alone, attacked, rejected, forsaken, hopeless and helpless. I felt a sense of urgency to get away.

I told my husband, "I'm leaving with or without you."

I could take no more of the pain. I knew what their reason was for excommunicating Mark, but what was their reason for excommunicating me? He was the one that went to jail, not me. I had to believe it was all in His sovereign plan.

Mark went to town and talked to an acquaintance about renting one of his apartments for the time being, until we could get ourselves on our feet again. And he agreed.

Chapter 17

So we moved ourselves and our five boys into a one-bedroom apartment in town. Imagine that! Seven people in a tiny one-bedroom apartment with no communication with the rest of our world. We had no money, no phone, neither one of us had a driver's license. We had no transportation since we couldn't keep a horse and buggy in town. It was absolutely devastating.

My husband glared at me and said, "Just look what you got us into!"

And at that moment I believed that it was all my fault. It was one of the most devastating moments of my life. I asked myself, "What did I get us into?"

I threw myself across the bed and sobbed my heart out. Where would we go from here? How would we pick up the pieces of this broken, shattered world of ours? We left everything we had ever known, our whole world, friends, family, acquaintances and ventured out into a new, uncharted territory. And we just did not know how to do this.

How does a person start a new life with so little? There was very little to work with. I walked up town to the pay phone, dropped in a quarter and called my friend Sharon. She was my anchor. My lifeline. My guidance. Where would I be without her? Since Mark had been charged with multiple charges, including driving without a license, the courts ordered him to go to alcohol counseling for a whole year. He would not be able to get his driver's license until this was completed since he was driving illegally without a driver's license.

"Truly all things work together for good to those who love the Lord and are called according to his purpose." -Romans 8:28 (KJV)

This whole thing was a blessing in disguise. Maybe, just maybe, Mark would get help with his alcohol addiction through the mandatory counseling and AA. At least he would be forced to stay sober for a year.

Sharon came over one day and said, "You need to drive my car. Practice your driving and parking so that you can go get your driver's license." And so I did. She then took me to the license branch where I passed the written and driver's exam.

How thrilled and excited I was. I felt liberated. And now for a vehicle. Now I needed a car. How was all this going to happen? I once again took it to the Lord.

Mark and one of his non-Amish employees started back to work. No crew. Just the two of them, which brought in some desperately needed funds. It helped that he couldn't drink. That really helped a lot. He was forced to stay sober and face reality.

He needed to realize that not everything that went wrong was my fault. He needed to stop shifting the blame onto my shoulders and start being accountable. And I needed to stop accepting the blame and stop enabling him.

This was hard. It was all new to me. I didn't realize how very dysfunctional we really were.

I missed my mom, my sisters, my whole world. This was excruciating. I knew how much they must be hurting as well. And I could not go see them and they would not come and see me.

Oh, dear God. All this pain over spiritual decisions. Why? Why? Why? Was all this pain necessary? It should not have been this hard. Why could they not understand? Where in scripture does it say I have to be Amish or go to hell?

Everyone had their own interpretation of scripture. This was all so confusing. As people from other churches found out we had left the Amish, they flocked to our door, each one trying to convince us that their church was the right one, and if we didn't come to their church we would be misled.

Oh, dear God, such confusion.

I prayed, "Lord, lead, guide and direct my path. Help me to follow in your footsteps." Starting over in a whole new world was a daunting task. But little by little, one step at a time, we did just that.

Our former neighbors Ed and Judy found us a very inexpensive car. We bought it from one of their family members. This was an unforgettable day. We had one of our Assembly friends come and babysit our boys while we went and bought the car, an Oldsmobile. It wasn't much, but to me it seemed like a dream come true.

I was now a licensed driver and the owner of a vehicle. This felt like freedom to me until I went to take my babysitter home. I was driving on the highway for the first time without an instructor when all of a sudden, the engine stopped, the lights turned off.

I was horrified. What is going on? I drifted off the road onto the shoulder of the highway and asked God to send a police officer, since I had no phone and no way to call anyone. As I glanced in my rear-view mirror, I saw flashing lights approaching.

An answer to prayer. I was so relieved.

The officers were kind. They called the tow truck and then took my babysitter home and me back to my apartment. I told them I may just have to go back to driving a horse and buggy. This transition was extremely hard.

Being shunned is so very harsh. There is no love in it whatsoever. It feels like pure hate. How in the world is pushing us away supposed to make us want to come back? From the day we were excommunicated, we were pushed out. There were no more family gatherings. No more going home to my mom's with my sisters.

I often wondered if they hurt as much as I did. At least they still had each other. Each time I went out into the public I felt ostracized.

My friend Sharon could not believe how I was treated by the Amish. She saw it first hand when she went to the grocery store with me. I was minding my own business, shopping for groceries when some Amish people started following me up one aisle and down another, glaring at me as if I had committed an unforgivable sin.

This is so wrong on so many levels. But I knew if Jesus was hated and was willing to carry the cross, then I could too.

"Truly I can do all things through Christ who strengthens me" - Philippians 4:13 (KJV)

Chapter 18

Rejection is painful at any age, but it is crippling for a child. At the time of our transition or move into town, little Sebastian was in first grade. It was February. There were still three months of school. The news of us leaving the Amish church traveled at lightning speed.

Soon the rumors circulated through the school and Sebastian was at the receiving end of the backlash.

The Amish kids no longer wanted to play with him because he was no longer considered Amish, therefore they had to shun him. The English kids didn't want to accept him because he had been Amish. He endured ridicule, rejection, and name calling— names such as "clapes" and "half-breed."

Talk about devastation and pain in his little world. So hurtful! So cruel! So destructive! How I wished I could endure the pain for him. In his mind he had done something very bad when he was so totally innocent! How would he ever get past this and grow up to be a healthy young man?

One month passed and then another. We struggled in many ways, trying to adjust to a whole new world we knew nothing about, like learning how to dress in normal clothing instead of our Amish clothes which I had sewn.

I had no idea how to determine the sizes of kids' clothes in the stores. I had no fashion sense. I relied heavily on my friend Sharon who helped me learn these things and also did the honors of giving my boys their first non-Amish haircuts. These were the pains of transitioning from one world to another.

The apartment was so small. There was only one bedroom and it was a very small one at that. But at least we now had indoor plumbing. There was a bathtub with hot and cold running water! I had a kitchen sink with running water. I no longer needed to pump and carry in every drop we consumed. Now I had a refrigerator! No more sour milk and spoiled foods.

We had electricity. At the flip of a switch the lights came on. I no longer needed my kerosene lamps. There was a bathroom with an inside toilet. No more outhouse where the snakes would hide under little Wyatt's potty chair.

This was huge! This actually compensated for all the inconveniences of our tight living quarters.

"Yes," I thought, "We can do this."

But still, I missed my family. My heart throbbed from the pains of not being able to talk to my mom and my siblings. Oh, how it hurt. I felt like my very heart was being ripped right out of my chest. If only they knew how much I loved and missed them. If only they understood I never meant to hurt them. If only they realized that it really was God leading, guiding, and directing my steps.

If only, if only, if only.

But all of the if only's went unrealized. The bleeding hearts and pain was still there. I could not change their beliefs and opinions. All I could do was put one foot in front of the other, and keep following in His footsteps. Trusting that someday they would realize that I had to do this.

My little boys missed their cousins immensely. None of this made any sense to them. Why couldn't they still run and play with their little playmates? Why did Grandpa no longer come and hold them in his lap? No more playing hide and seek with him.

Why? Why? Why? This was so confusing, puzzling, and hurtful. They did not understand! What could I say to them that would ease the hurt and help them to understand that it had to be this way and that none of it was their fault?

I felt like a miserable failure. I wanted my boys to be happy and healthy individuals and it tore my heart right out of my chest to see the raw hurt in their eyes.

My brother took it upon himself to go against the rules of the church and came to visit. He came to check on us. He loved us enough to be willing to suffer the consequences, and for that I was very grateful.

I would never forget it. He would have preferred we had stayed in the Amish church, but even more than that he wanted us to be okay. He said that mom and dad would like us to come visit but that we were not allowed to drive into the driveway in our own vehicle. Either we hire a driver or park our car across the street.

Mark was not ready for this. He would not even consider stepping foot on their property, but didn't mind if I went. My love for my family and my desire to see them out-weighed the fear of rejection, so I drove out to my parents' house with a couple of my boys and obediently parked my car across the street.

As I walked up the driveway, my brother met me there and walked with me into the house where I was awkwardly greeted by more family members. How grateful I was for my brother's unconditional love for me. This melted my heart. He will never realize how much this meant to me.

The visit went as I expected. Awkward! Way too much awkward silence. My sisters and I were happy to see each other. I knew what they were thinking. They were hoping I would change my mind and come back into the Amish community and I was wishing they would understand that I was only trying my best to obey my Lord and Savior.

Oh, how I wished they could see that. I loved them with all my heart but I had to follow Jesus, not only for my sake, but for the sake of my children.

All too soon, it was time to go back to our apartment. I went to gather my little guys who were having a great time playing with their cousins. They had missed them immensely and did not want to leave.

"Do we have to go?" they asked. "We just got here. We are having fun. When can we come back? Can they come with us?"

Their young minds just could not comprehend all of this separation and why it couldn't be like it always was before.

Since we were literally starting over in life, we decided to buy a little home outside of the Amish community and enrolled the two oldest boys into a public school where there were no Amish kids. We felt it was the right thing to do for them, hoping to making the transition easier for them, somewhere new where no one knew they had been Amish. Hopefully they didn't need to experience the pain of being rejected.

Little by little, we began to adjust to our new way of living. I relied totally and completely on my Lord to lead, guide, and direct me, to help me live in obedience to Him. I depended on Him for everything. My faith in Him grew stronger each day. I grew spiritually and became very involved in the church that my friend Sharon introduced me to. Even though Mark did not share my enthusiasm for God and church, he seemed to adjust to our new life outside the Amish community and continued to go to alcohol counseling which helped him face reality.

Finally, I began to see answered prayers and I could see a much brighter future. I was happy to commit myself and my dear family into the hands of my dear Lord and Savior. I know I can trust Him completely to lead us into a future of life in Him. A surrendered life of victory. I look forward to continuing my story in the next book of our life in a whole new world. What an adventure.

Knowing my Heavenly Father was in control of myself, my family and my future, I could totally trust that whatever happens. I am never alone. He will never lead us in the wrong direction. I learned that I cannot lean on my own understanding or on the opinions and beliefs of people. I learned that we can go forward in life trusting that we will learn and grow as we hold the hand of our Savior. I walk in peace knowing I was doing all I knew to do for Him and for my family.

I was excited about the future and all that life has to offer a growing family of all boys. Knowing, trusting and believing they will grow up to be outstanding young men with a bright future ahead of them. So many possibilities! They would get to choose their career or vocation. They would get to follow their hearts, dreams and desires!

I couldn't wait to watch them spread their wings and fly.

I ventured out into the wilderness of life and made a happy life for me and my sons that I am proud of. Together we ended the cycle of alcoholism and abuse in our family. My sons lead full, joyful lives with their families.

I was a stay at home mom until my boys were grown and gone from home. I started studying reflexology and alternative health and preventative solutions in 1988 and have been treating people's feet ever since.

Currently am in a ladies' jail ministry and loving life. I am a full-time grandmother, insurance broker and encourager of those in need.

I am blessed beyond anything I could have imagined and I thoroughly enjoy life and love my friends and family.

I pray I am an encouragement to all who read my story.

*

Watch for book 2, coming soon!

About the Author:

I am first and foremost a child of the most high God! I have Forsaken all to follow Him. I am a sinner saved by His Amazing Grace!! When I was miserable and alone, He picked me up. When my sins were crimson red, on the cross for me He bled. How can I ever repay Him? I can't!! But I can tell the world how Amazing He is. And that is my ultimate goal.

I was born and raised Old Order Amish. I married an Amish man and we had 5 boys when we were excommunicated from the Amish church. I am now in a ladies' jail ministry, loving life.

I pray I am an encouragement to all who read my story.

Please follow me on Amazon to be notified when I release new books! Book 2 is coming soon.

Thank you for reading,

-Eirene Eicher

13084045R00055

Made in the
USA
Monee, IL